# Return of Old Maine Woman

---

## Tales of Growing Up and Getting Older

*by Glenna Johnson Smith*

Also from Islandport Press

*Where Cool Waters Flow*
by Randy Spencer

*My Life in the Maine Woods*
by Annette Jackson

*Nine Mile Bridge*
by Helen Hamlin

*Shoutin' into the Fog*
by Thomas Hanna

*In Maine*
by John N. Cole

*The Cows Are Out*
by Trudy Chambers Price

*Hauling by Hand*
by Dean Lawrence Lunt

*Suddenly the Cider Didn't Taste So Good*
by John Ford

*Finding Your Inner Moose*
by Susan Poulin

# Return of Old Maine Woman

Tales of Growing Up and
Getting Older

*by Glenna Johnson Smith*

ISLANDPORT PRESS

Islandport Press
P.O. Box 10
Yarmouth, Maine 04096
www.islandportpress.com
books@islandportpress.com

ISBN: 978-1-939017-30-7
Library of Congress Card Number: 2013922655

Publisher: Dean L. Lunt
Book jacket design by Karen F. Hoots, Hoots Design
Book designed by Michelle A. Lunt, Islandport Press
Cover image of Glenna Johnson Smith courtesy of
    the author
Cover backdrop image courtesy of Dean L. Lunt

*With love to Steve, Barney, and Mel,*
*and to the women in my family:*
*Ashley, Diane, Hillary, Jasmine,*
*Linda, Lorraine, Shirley,*
*and Sylvia.*

# Acknowledgments

There's a line from a song I recall: "I get by with a little help from my friends."

I get by with a great amount of help and encouragement from family and friends. As I grow older, I find it harder to have faith in myself; yet, the loving support from my sons, granddaughters, and nieces, and approval from dear friends, keeps me going.

First, without the constant encouragement of Kathryn Olmstead, *Echoes* editor, I would have had nothing published. Assistant editor at *Echoes*, Mary-Anne McHugh, has helped and supported me in more ways than I can list.

I'm sure the readers and friends who send notes don't realize how much they are responsible for keeping me writing, observing, and enjoying each day. Please, all of you, accept my gratitude, my daily thank-yous.

My love to all of you,

Glenna

# Contents

# Foreword

*by Kathryn Olmstead*

If Glenna Johnson Smith's ideas about aging catch on, cosmetic companies and plastic surgeons could be in trouble. At ninety-four, Glenna has long affirmed the value of being old, contradicting the norms of a culture infatuated with youth.

"Growing old is not a disease or a disgrace; it's just a stage of life," she says. "I haven't seen a decade yet that did not have something good to offer."

After she retired from the faculty of Presque Isle High School at age seventy, Glenna began writing a column for *Echoes* magazine in Aroostook County. As we discussed a name for the column, she insisted it contain the word *old*, and settled on "Old County Woman."

"I like the sound of the words *old woman*," she wrote in defense of her decision. "They're strong words—earthy, honest. I'm grateful I've survived long enough to label myself with them."

Glenna always thought she would retire to the coastal village where she grew up in Hancock County. But at some point she realized she was a County woman. In the years after she arrived in Aroostook County as a bride in 1941, she came to appreciate the way the vast fields meet the sky at the horizon. That landscape became part of her identity. Even though her essays immortalize her hometown of Ashville, with its nearby summer people and small-town traditions, it is Aroostook that defines who Glenna has become.

As you'll read in this collection, her writing reveals that young people and women were not allowed to express themselves freely when she was growing up. Like other women of her generation, Glenna's mother suppressed her own opinions and deferred to men. But Glenna eventually came to envision a world where people would not be imprisoned by social expectations.

Attending a workshop for teachers held on the West Coast was a turning point. Glenna was surprised when the leader viewed her as independent and willing to buck convention. She was empowered by this acceptance of her nonconformity, and brought that message back to her classroom.

"She told her students to persevere, to reach deeply, and to use writing as a means toward self-discovery and growth," wrote a former student in a tribute published in 1998. "She did not tell us what to think, but how, and she'd congratulate us on what we had done right, rather than inking us to death on what we'd done wrong. Along with her desire to bring out our true selves through writing, she tapped the little bud of confidence we each had within ourselves and transformed it into a bouquet."

Former students continue to express their appreciation for Glenna's affirmation of their individuality. She will never know how many adults are more productive and satisfied with their lives because she convinced them it was okay to express their beliefs honestly, even if they were different from their peers.

And so, it is not surprising that at age seventy, Glenna embraced the words *old woman*. Fed up with condescending, demeaning stereotypes and silly euphemisms for "old," she set out to make the term positive instead of pejorative. As the years passed, she chronicled her own experiences with humor, tenderness, and insight, enchanting readers of all ages.

She is annoyed by the use of *old woman* as an insult. A man laments that he cried "like an old woman" watching a movie, or a baseball coach berates a player for throwing the ball "like an old woman." She is tired of seeing television portrayals of stupid elderly women who must be set straight by a young person.

"*Old* isn't always a bad word," she says. "Old furniture is valued, old stories are retold—old things gain luster for being old."

She wonders at the well-meaning people who greet her as a "young lady" or introduce her as "ninety years young," observing that "in their mistaken way," they think she wants to be young.

"And why shouldn't they?" she asks. "Look at the billions of dollars being spent on things to make you look young." In a culture where women and men try to disguise their age with everything from hair color to plastic surgery, Glenna presents a clear alternative. Instead of fighting and fearing old age, she uses her years as fodder for creative activity that continues to awaken new discoveries.

"With the structure of my working years gone, I have enjoyed the freedom to make my own decisions." Her choices have kept her young.

In these essays, Glenna is not just giving a voice to older people; she is also demonstrating for the next generation a new way to grow old. Imagine the effect on our culture if more of us followed her example.

"Listen to the words *old woman*, or *old man*," she says to young people. "They don't sound so bad, do they? With a little luck, and by the grace of God, you'll be one of us someday."

—Kathryn Olmstead, editor
*Echoes* Magazine, 2013

# Prologue: My Spot

I HAPPEN TO LIVE AT THE CENTER of the universe. From here I can branch out to all of Presque Isle, then Aroostook County, State of Maine, New England, USA, North America, world, universe—all in a row. I'm lucky I don't live in some out-of-the-way place. You need proof of the superiority of my spot? I'll give you proof.

From my old rocking chair I see a most unusual tree; it's tall, goes way above the telephone wires, and the right-hand side of the tree is pine, the left side is spruce. If you want to get picky you can find two trunks in there someplace, but what I see is one perfectly symmetrical tree. Both sides are waving at the wind. I like to watch them swaying against the winter-gray sky. The very tip—spruce, I think—is uninhabited at present, but often it contains one of my crow friends discoursing on the evils of the day. Now I ask you, how many people have such a tree?

And that's not all. Perhaps two-thirds of the way to the top—too high for a kid, or even for an adult to have placed it there, unless he were riding in the bucket of a cherry picker— is an unidentified object. Sometimes it looks like a fat hen or duck, but since it hasn't moved for years, I guess it's not alive. Often it looks like a little church with a steeple, or a head with a pointy hat. When the sun hits it, the thing turns a reddish-brown shade not seen anywhere else on the tree. I ask people who have better eyes than mine—none can name it. I'd try my binoculars, but one granddaughter, when she was little, dropped them, and they haven't been the same since.

Yesterday at sunset a shaft of light hit that spot. It looked like a young man wearing sunglasses. I know that someday I will find the true answer.

When a friend calls and asks what I am doing, I say "Oh, nothing." It would take too long to explain about the thing in the tree.

Then on a pole to the right of the tree there is a wondrous light, my own private moon that doesn't wax, wane, or rotate. I am ever so grateful to the city of Presque Isle for it; it enables me to go all over the house at night without flipping a switch. The neighbors may think I'm sleeping, but I may be having an adventure—watching the path of a star, or wondering what would happen to me, where I'd end up, if that plane that flew so low on its way to the airfield had hit my house. Although I wouldn't have the expense of a long-lasting illness, it sure would mess up the neighborhood.

My biggest-of-all mystery: Once, at two o'clock in the morning, I was sitting and staring out an upstairs window when suddenly there was a bright and blinding light which passed instantly. The next day I made calls to see if anyone else had reported it—if there had been a meteor shower, perhaps—and found nothing. Still, I knew I hadn't imagined it. A few weeks later I heard of a couple who were returning from a late party that night and also saw a brilliant light.

From my window I have watched little girls with doll carriage parades, little boys with bats and balls and skateboards. They're all grown-up now and the street is too quiet. And in all those years, not one baseball came through my big front window. So many miracles.

I've watched crows stop and look both ways before marching across the road—as if they've forgotten how to fly.

I've watched my cat Coty chase a squirrel who then climbed a tree. Then Coty climbed the tree, couldn't get down, and wailed until a man came with a ladder.

One day a moose walked down our street. I didn't see him, but the neighbors told me. Sometimes Sheila and Mike have a party under the trees and we all go. The maples on the street are so bright in the fall that the sun seems to shine all the time.

And all that raking—and kids jumping into piles of leaves.

One night when I walked to the end of the street and back before going to bed, I saw a shooting star go halfway across the sky. I knew that was a good omen.

Downstate friends who look out at the bay, islands, and a mountain tell me they're sorry I don't have a view.

What, me—here at the center of the world? No view?

# Part One:

# Growing Up

# 1

# Twelve

ALL THAT SUMMER I WONDERED who I was. I was no longer the little girl with the long curls and the perky white sailor dress Mama had made; no longer the girl who climbed the pine tree, pretending it was the mast of her schooner, or sometimes, her pirate ship.

That happy little girl had left unhappy changes in her place. Edna and Leola, two older girls who were my heroes, had sometimes let me drift along in their wake. Now in high school, they had summer jobs, they dated boys, and they went to the Saturday-night dances. I felt they were years away from me.

Yet there were worse changes. One day Papa took me to his barber, who chopped off my curls, leaving a mess that stuck out in all directions. Never again would people see me and say, "Look at her pretty curls." On top of all that, I took a growing spurt and shot up taller than the kids my age. I was skinny and gawky. I tried to slump over so I wouldn't look so tall, but then Grammie would tell me to straighten my back. The little girl who loved to run through hay fields and along rocky shores now fell over her own feet.

Moreover, the pretty dresses Mama had made no longer fit. She tried to alter hand-me-downs, but they all hung limp as dishrags. Then one frightening day I showed Mama my bloomers and she said, "You're a woman now." After groaning through the cramps and after being tired all the time, I didn't really want to be a woman.

In addition to these woes, I found I needed glasses because I squinted. The eye doctor chose round spectacles with wide black frames. They pinched my ears and my nose, and when I looked in the mirror I saw a pale scarecrow with big owly eyes. I tried to be invisible when people were around.

Sometimes that summer I picked berries for Mama, but more often I went to a secret place outdoors and read. Mama sold magazines outside the post office cubicle in the old store where we lived. She was told to save a piece of the covers of magazines that didn't sell, and discard the rest. Often I could salvage copies of movie magazines, *True Story* and *True Romance*, and hide them in my special place. Mama's ethics wouldn't allow her to give the magazines away, although some people asked for them. The same ethics made her say I could not read them, but I don't think she checked up carefully. At least, she never caught me with my stash.

Mama's days were so busy, with tending garden, doing the laundry by hand, cooking good meals for Papa and me, and running the post office, that there was little time for sleuthing. While she was busy I would run away to my magazines and devour stories of beautiful women and handsome men who had mildly steamy love affairs filled with gigantic problems, but who finally married and lived happily ever after.

Yet I couldn't make myself believe that these characters had anything to do with real life. The marriages I observed didn't look so great. As I hid in the post office and eavesdropped, I heard more complaints than compliments:

8

"He makes me so mad. I just get the floors all scrubbed when he tracks mud all over them. He says he's too busy to wipe his feet before he comes in."

"I hate his smelly pipe. I make him smoke in the barn."

The men complained, too:

"I wish she wouldn't mess up the *Daily* and cut things out before I get to read it."

"Supper was late again last night. She was off somewhere with her sister."

It didn't take me long to figure out that I didn't want to get married. But why should I worry? Homely as I was, no man would ever propose to me.

Then one Sunday afternoon Papa took Mama and me along when he visited his older friend, Bill. I think he liked Bill partly because he was a fellow Lodge member, and partly because he told great stories of all the places he'd visited and all the jobs he'd had. I think Mama and Bill's wife—I can't recall her name—liked each other, too. They had one thing in common—each rushed to meet her husband's needs before he knew he needed anything. While we were sitting on their porch, Bill's wife said, "Are you cold, dear? Shall I bring you your brown sweater? Would you like a cup of coffee?" Bill waved away both offers, and continued telling Papa his tales.

Just as I was getting good and bored, Bill's son, his wife, and their little daughter dropped by. I've forgotten their names, too, but I thought they were the most beautiful family I'd ever seen. The husband and wife were obviously in love, for they laughed, kidded each other, hugged and kissed right there for all to see. Both of them doted on the little girl, who had dark curls and shining blue eyes. I was pleased when she came over to me and started jabbering. I had always wanted a baby sister, but whenever I made that request to Mama, she gave me a look that said that was the last thing on God's good green earth that she wanted.

The baby's name may have been Mary something. Maybe Mary Sue. Anyway, I'll call her that. Her mother said I could take her out on the lawn if I wanted to. Mary Sue took my hand, eager to go. We walked around the flower garden, and I showed her the spit under some of the daisy petals. I put some of it on her arm, and mine, and we watched the tiny grasshoppers crawl out of the foam. Then we laughed at butterflies and we saw a little toad. I made up stories about Mr. Toad and Mrs. Butterfly. She kept saying, "More 'tory." When her parents came out and told her she had to go now, she took my hand and said, "I 'tay here." I don't know when I'd felt so happy. She didn't even care that I looked like an owl.

Next day at the post office Mama told an older woman that we had visited Bill and his family. The woman laughed and said she knew Bill when they were young. She said he was a wild one who chased women all the time, and that his dear wife never let on that she knew. Mama said she hoped nobody told Seth about that, for he'd never believe anything bad about his friend.

I wasn't interested in what Bill had done, but Mary Sue's parents became my heroes, and I decided maybe marriage could be wonderful after all. I was sure I would love to have a little daughter like Mary Sue. When a few days later the young wife called Mama and asked if I would like to spend a day with her, I was excited. Since they were Bill's family, Papa was glad to drive me the few miles to their house. He asked the wife when he should pick me up, and she said not until after supper.

I loved their tiny house. The wife—I'll call her Helen—kept it looking perfect, like a dollhouse. While she worked in her garden I played outdoors with Mary Sue. Later when she went in to do some cooking, I read to Mary Sue in the living room. We ate lunch on the little porch, and while I snapped beans for supper I told stories to the baby.

"You are so good with her," Helen said. "I hope you will come over often." I told her I would love to.

Helen said Mary Sue could take her nap on the couch if I would lie down beside her so she wouldn't roll off. I watched the sleeping child and then I looked into a corner of the kitchen and watched Helen bake a cake. It had three layers, and she covered it with brown-sugar boiled frosting. Then she washed her cooking dishes and polished the sideboard. There was nothing on it but a blue vase with wild roses and the cake, which looked like a picture in *Ladies' Home Journal.*

Before it was time for her husband to return home, Helen changed her blouse and skirt, brushed her long dark hair, and splashed on some cologne. From the couch I could see her coming and going to the bedroom, humming and smiling. Oh, how I wanted to grow up and be a wife!

When her husband came in, they hugged and kissed. Then he looked at the cake and said, "Wow! What's the occasion?"

She laughed. "Can't I make a cake for my man any old time?" He kissed her again. Then she told him supper was almost ready, but that she was going to the garden for a few more things for the salad.

When she went out the door he came into the living room, looked down at his sleeping daughter, then bent close to me and whispered, "Hello, pretty girl." For a moment I was flattered. I couldn't imagine anyone calling me a pretty girl.

Then he kissed me hard on the mouth. I was scared, and also shocked that my idea of the perfect husband and father would do such a thing. I couldn't think what to do or say. Then over his shoulder I saw Helen looking at us. She looked sick—or perhaps sad. When she knew that I saw her, she drew back into the kitchen.

Then Mary Sue opened her eyes. Her daddy picked her up, hugged her, and said, "How's my little pumpkin?" Helen came in smiling, and said, "You know what I'd like? A ride; it's so nice out. Let's give Glenna a ride home so Seth won't have to drive over."

"Before supper?" the husband asked.

"I feel guilty keeping her so long," Helen said. "Kathleen would probably like to have her home for supper."

On the way he told Helen what he'd been doing at work. She said little. He asked, "Are you feeling okay? You look a little tired."

She smiled at him. "I guess I weeded too long in the hot sun."

When we drove in at my house I hugged Mary Sue, who was sitting with me in the backseat. She said, "No! 'Tay in car!" I thanked Helen for inviting me. She smiled, but said nothing. They drove away, and Mama asked how come I was home before supper. I told her what Helen said.

"Well, I am glad you're here," she said. "We're having things you like—haddock chowder, cabbage salad, hot biscuits, raspberry pie."

I couldn't eat much, though. When Mama asked if I'd been filling up on candy, I told her we'd had a big lunch.

I felt awful and didn't sleep well that night. Did Helen think that kiss was my idea? Did I do something really bad?

12

Helen didn't invite me again, and later I heard Papa tell Mama that they had moved away. The husband had been offered a good job in his field, so they had moved to New Jersey. I never saw them again.

I often thought about Mary Sue, though. I hoped she grew up happy in a home where her parents loved each other. I hoped her daddy didn't make a habit of kissing young girls after telling them they were pretty. For a long time I had guilty feelings whenever I thought of them, and wondered what I should have done. I still wonder sometimes.

# 2

# John and Priscilla

I HAVE AN OLD DINNER PLATE of great value. The
once-white background is now crackled, stained, and chipped.
Around its twelve-sided edge there's a dull blue stripe which
may have been painted by a tired worker with a shaky hand.
In the center of the plate there is a scene with the title PILGRIM
SERIES. A man and a woman are standing on a hill looking out
at woods, fields, a winding brook, and what may be a bay.
Another woman is sitting on a rock, also gazing out at the
scene. All are wearing the Pilgrim clothes seen in schoolbooks
when I was a child. I was told that the couple was John Alden
and Priscilla, whom I also knew from my school reader. I think
my plate is the last remaining dish from my grandmother
Johnson's set, but I remember some of the other plates, each
of which had a different picture. In one, John is holding the
skein while Priscilla winds a ball of yarn. In another they are
sitting by the fire and holding hands. That was my favorite.
Sometimes they were eating a meal; on one they were walking
to church. I recall that sometimes I gulped my food so I could
see what was happening on my plate.

There were imperfections in the enamel. Today we'd call
such a dish a "second," and we'd expect to buy it for half-price.
I'm sure the set cost little when it was new. My relatives were
all poor in money income in the 1930s, but they worked hard

to provide good food, warm clothes, and safe, comfortable houses for their families.

I'm not sure where the dishes came from. Grammie spoke of some dishes coming from Marblehead, the destination of the schooner on which Grampie put out to sea for many seasons. The schooner—I think it was called the *Mary Augustus*—carried granite for city street paving blocks, and returned with a cargo of manufactured goods. When he returned home, Reuel Johnson, my grandfather, always brought a gift to his wife, Annie. The Pilgrim set may have been one of his gifts.

Yet there is another possibility. Grammie told me that sometimes local storekeepers gave dishes with a purchase—a free plate with a bag of flour, for instance. How exciting it would have been to see what picture came with the next purchase. It was said that Gippie Hanna, who owned the general store, never told a customer that he was out of the goods they requested. He would take down his spyglass, squint out over the bay, and say, "Schooner will be coming around the island anytime now. It'll be on it, all right."

Grammie and her three little sons, as well as other families in the village, also watched for the boat to come around the island. Once it had sailed out of sight, there was no news until those sails appeared, headed for the home port perhaps many weeks later. There was always the dread of storms at sea taking ship and crew away forever. Everyone recognized the shape and the sails of each schooner. When the *Mary Augustus* came into view, Gram and her sons would rush to the pier.

I wonder if Annie's happiness at the safe return of her husband was somewhat tempered with her being left behind to milk the cow, feed the chickens, carry the wood, tend the garden, and care for her sons. She worried most about her second son, Henry, who had terrible bouts with asthma. I like to think my dish rode on one of those trips, that it was Grampie's gift, or that it came later, a dish with each bag of flour from Gippie's store. I hope Annie loved those dishes.

I look at my plate and see baked beans and brown bread with homemade pickles for Saturday-night supper. I see a noon dinner of baked haddock, mashed potatoes, carrots, and hot biscuits. Dessert might have been hot gingerbread or pumpkin pie. I see the plate washed in the pantry in sudsy water from a big cake of Fels-Naptha soap. I see it rinsed with boiling water from the teakettle, dried with a linen dish towel, and placed in the cupboard as carefully as if it had been crafted by Spode or Wedgwood. Although a dealer of antiques would pay little—if anything—for my worn, chipped plate, it is worth thousands to me—thousands of Grammie's good breakfasts, dinners, and suppers, thousands of daydreams in my bed at night (mostly love stories about John and Priscilla), thousands of childhood hours in the old farmhouse beside the bay.

# 3

# The Old Witch

I WAS TERRIFIED OF Aunt Tune, who wasn't really my aunt. (In Ashville we always called old people "aunt" and "uncle.") And she never did me any harm. It was the way she looked: tall, straight, thin, and scowling. She dressed all in black—always in a long black skirt that blew in the wind when she strode across the ridge behind the post office where I lived. I was sure that if she raised her bony arms she could just fly away—no broom or anything.

Aunt Tune, whose real name was Eunice, lived with Uncle Asa—we pronounced it *Asey*—in a tiny, weather-beaten hut across the ridge and down by the shore. All I remember of Uncle Asa is that he was bent and his face was brown and leathery. I know that he fished and dug clams for a living, and that as long as he lived he did all their errands in the village, while Aunt Tune seldom left her house. It was after his death that I became afraid of her, an ancient crone living alone in a shack that looked like a fairy-tale hut where a wicked witch would catch, cook, and eat little children. Like me.

In spite of my fear of her, though, I loved her house, because there was a tall lilac bush on either side—a white one on the left, a purple one on the right. Their flowering branches met over the low roof. Sometimes I daydreamed that Aunt Tune would die or fly away and I would live my life there under the lilac trees and close to the shore.

19

Yet she lived on, and while I played on the ridge I listened for the heavy tread of her boots and the swish of her skirt. When I suspected she was approaching I hid in the alder bushes and tried to hold my breath until she passed. If she caught sight of me she would mutter, "Pesky yar one," and I would almost die of fright. Because she could neither read nor write, many of her words were of her own making. Children were often called young ones, yet the term was seldom used as a compliment. "Their house is so full of young ones you'd fall over one of the little pests if you went in." Often to my mother Aunt Tune would say, "Can't you make your pesky yar one behave?"

Every day Tune walked across the ridge to visit the post office. She received no mail and bought neither newspapers nor magazines. I can't recall ever seeing her in the grocery store, the church, or in any other house. She came to use the telephone—one of the few in the village. She always called her only niece that she knew of. The conversation went something like this: "Hello, Edith? How are you today?" Pause for a one-word answer. "How is your husband?" Pause. "How is little Jerry?" Pause. "How is little Nellie?" Pause. "That's good. Good-bye."

Because of her lack of travel and schooling, Aunt Tune thought there were only two places: here and away. She lived here. Edith lived away. One day a woman at the post office mentioned she'd been away for a few days. Aunt Tune asked, "And did you see Edith?" I wondered if Edith and her family ever visited Aunt Tune or took her for a ride. She never mentioned seeing them.

My fear was so strong that I often encountered Aunt Tune in my nightmares. I'd be running home across the ridge, her long strides gaining on me. I'd reach the kitchen door, but my fist would freeze on the knob. My parents were sitting inside in the lamplight, but I couldn't call out to them. Then Aunt Tune would be upon me, her wrinkled beak just inches from my face, her scrawny claws closing around my neck. When I'd wake up screaming, Mama would come into my room and say, "There, there now, there's nothing to be afraid of. Go back to sleep." She would tuck me in and I would try to stay awake so I wouldn't have another visit from the witch.

On her way to the post office Aunt Tune had to walk past our outhouse, which was behind the barn, across from the big old dry goods store turned into a post office. It was a long walk. I always hooked the door when I went in, for I was sure Aunt Tune would find me there someday and do me in. If it were not for my fear, I would have liked the place. Mama had covered the walls with works of art—soon faded and fly-specked: *The Blue Boy*, cows grazing in a pasture, and a sad old Indian. She had cut them from calendars. Old Sears Roebuck catalogs doubled as toilet tissue and reading material. I would listen long for Aunt Tune before I would dare to unhook the door and leave the outhouse.

What little I know of Aunt Tune's past I learned one rainy day when I was hiding behind a counter and eavesdropping on the people who came for their mail. One woman said Aunt Tune was from a town several miles away, where she was born into a big and poor family. When Asa said he would marry their thirteen-year-old daughter, they willingly gave her to him. I wonder now about many things. What was her life like with Asa? Who or what supported her after Uncle Asa's death? I know that my mother often took her whole meals, and also gave her cookies or a piece of cake to take home after her visits. I couldn't imagine why Mama was so kind to her, since the witch would surely tear me up into little pieces and eat me someday. I remember there was some kind of old age pension back then. Maybe Aunt Tune received that, or perhaps she was supported by the town. I think men in the village cut and piled wood for her kitchen stove, which heated her house. I'm sure other neighbors took food to her, and perhaps summer people gave her boxes of clothing. There are many questions I wish I had asked my mother.

I remember my horror on a day when Mama handed me a covered pail and said, "I want you to take this down to Aunt Tune."

I said, "You take it, Mama. My stomach aches."

"I can't leave because it's almost mail time," Mama said. "Aunt Tune didn't look good yesterday, and she hasn't been over yet today. I want her to have this thermos of fish chowder while it's still hot. There's a little jar of applesauce, too, and some biscuits and a piece of pie. Don't drop it or swing it around."

"I can't go." I said. "I'm sick."

"You stop your foolishness right this minute, young lady, or your father will hear about this. You know what you'll get then."

My fear of being spanked with Papa's leather slipper was right up there with my fear of Aunt Tune, so I started out.

"Don't drag your feet," Mama said.

As I neared the little house I looked around to see if Aunt Tune might be outdoors. She wasn't. I stood on her doorstep for what seemed to me like hours, getting the courage to knock. I really did have a stomachache. Finally I set the pail down, rapped hard on the door, and ran when I heard her footsteps. She opened the door and called, "What's this?"

"Mama sent it," I yelled. I didn't stop running until I was out of her sight and out of breath. Later she complained to Mama that she had wanted me to do an errand and I wouldn't stop. Mama told me that Aunt Tune was just a poor, pitiful old woman who should be treated with kindness. Her message was wasted on me.

Although I thought she must be a hundred years old when I was five, Aunt Tune lived long after I grew up and moved to Aroostook County. Mama told me that she visited Aunt Tune one day and found her in bed and very ill. Mama fed her a little soup and then told her she needed to see the doctor. "I'll call him," Mama said.

"No!" Aunt Tune said. "No man has ever seen my bare body, and no man is going to. I'll just die right here in my bed." Later I heard Mama say that if Uncle Asa had never seen her bare body, that might have something to do with their never having had any children.

Mama and the neighbors kept her as comfortable as they could. She died a few days later.

I often think about Aunt Tune. Along with recalling my terror, I feel sad for a little girl whose family gave her away to a stranger and who lived out her life with no knowledge of anything beyond the cabin under the lilac trees and a niece from away.

# 4

# My Wild Night

YESTERDAY A FRIEND AND I REMEMBERED how back in our childhood, we were both persuaded that going to bed without washing our faces and brushing our teeth would be a serious impropriety. That led to my remembering the one night when I observed neither of these strictures—partly because I didn't go to bed, and partly because there was no water available. More serious than breaking the rules of cleanliness, I could have been suspended from the University of Maine for that night's events.

Rules concerning girls were rigidly enforced in the 1930s and '40s, and our dean followed those rules. I will never forget my interview with her when I applied for a job waiting on tables. She asked, "Do you bathe daily? Do you use deodorant? Do you wear a clean bra? Slip? Stockings? Underpants?" I don't think she believed my answers. I never in my life felt so inferior or so unclean. I wish I could have known then that a year later, Bill Wells, head of Food Services, would often choose me to wait on the head table at banquets and reunions. As far as I can remember, I never dropped a tray or mixed up an order. Although I felt inferior in most areas of college life, I was proud of my ability as a waitress.

During April college break in my junior year I went with my boyfriend, Don Smith, then a senior, to visit with his family in Easton. It was a warm April even for Aroostook; there were traces of snow, but also green grass, and in sheltered places, a few crocuses and daffodils. Don and I rode from Orono to Easton with friends of his, and we planned to ride back with them. During the week, however, an elderly couple, friends of the family, asked if we would ride with them. I've forgotten their names, so I'll call them Bob and Ellen. Bob wanted help with the driving, partly because he was worried about Ellen, who had fallen ill during their visit to Aroostook County relatives.

We started at about noon on a warm sunny day. I was to sign in at my dorm by nine that night, but we would arrive earlier, in time for me to wait on tables for the Sunday-evening meal. Don enjoyed driving the big car—perhaps a Buick. Bob sat in front with him, Ellen and me in the backseat. She, with her pillow and partially reclining, said she was comfortable. I think we all enjoyed the ride. When we reached the Haynesville woods, we noticed little spits of snow. We laughed. Imagine snow on this beautiful spring day! Don joked that he was good at shoveling, and Bob said there was a shovel right in the trunk.

All too soon the snow was beating down and the wind was howling. Don couldn't see ahead, and there was so little traffic that nobody had made a track for us. Soon little drifts appeared in the road. For a while Don would speed up and we would fly through them. Finally, though, a drift stopped us, and Don had to shovel.

After that we had to stop more often, and the snowdrifts grew bigger. Don, a college athlete, was in such good condition that he could keep up this pace without getting too tired, but our progress became slower and slower.

It was dark before we reached Macwahoc, where we were forced to stop because there were cars and a bus in the road.

When we learned that the road to Bangor was closed, Bob said we'd stay at a nearby motel. It turned out that the bus and car passengers before us had filled the motel, along with the spare rooms and couches in the few houses in the village. We would have to spend the night in the car, or in the filling station.

Since the weather had turned cold, we tried the filling station, a small, smelly, greasy place. The old man who ran it was also dirty and greasy, and obviously annoyed at our request, but he agreed that we could stay there. When we told him of Ellen's illness, he brought from his living quarters behind the station room some old coats and dirty blankets which we fashioned into a makeshift bed for Ellen on the floor, near the woodstove. Luckily she had her pillow from the car. We had all been hungry for some time, but there was no store or restaurant within walking distance, so we made do with what was available in our shelter for the night: candy bars and soft drinks. We could smell food and coffee from the man's kitchen out back, but he offered nothing. There were no chairs in the room, so Don and Bob sat on the woodpile and I sat across the room, on a red Coca-Cola cooler. There wasn't room to lie down on it, but at least it was up from the drafty floor.

The night dragged on. Ellen slept some of the time, and she never complained, although we all knew she was uncomfortable. Don, Bob, and I made frequent trips to the window, hoping to see a snowplow. From time to time, Don put wood in the stove. The owner didn't ever come out to check on us. I've tried to think what served as our toilet; I know we were not invited into the owner's quarters. Perhaps there was an outhouse. Perhaps we went in the snow.

For breakfast we had Hershey bars and Coke. When the sky grew lighter, we watched and waited. It was nearly noon before a state plow appeared and the road was opened. Dirty, tired, and hungry for real food, we started on our way—after Don had shoveled the car out of a snowbank.

My roommate laughed when I returned to the dorm. I hadn't realized how dirty my face was, and how rumpled my hair. A shower and the clean sheets on my cot had never felt so good. Since I had missed my only afternoon class, I slept until it was time to report for work in the dining room.

When I got there I learned that I was in real trouble. Next day I must go before a person who terrified me, the dean of women, and the student council to learn my punishment for failing to sign in at the proper time. I assumed that when I explained what had happened, I would be released. Not so. The dean believed that I was off somewhere spending the night with my boyfriend. And so I was—he on the woodpile, I on the Coke cooler. Finally a girl from my dorm testified that she had seen me drive up in a car containing an elderly couple. We had dropped Don off on the way, at his frat house. At last I was freed of blame, but only after many long, frightening minutes.

I suspect that the dean gave in only because Don was a big man on campus and highly respected. If I, an unknown, had had an unknown boyfriend, I may well have been suspended. Almost seventy-one years have passed since my wild night. Don and I married and became potato farmers. We both taught school to pay the bills; the farm was heavily mortgaged when Don's grandfather, John Calvin Smith, handed it over to us. The best thing we did there was raise our three sons. Life has been good to me. I'm glad, however, that it has been predictable enough in good times or bad for me to wash my face and brush my teeth before I retire.

# 5

# Frozen in Time

WHEN A FRIEND BROUGHT me an Easton High School faculty picture from the 1959 yearbook, I stared at it until I was back a half-century ago in a different land, a different era. Although we look serious in the picture, every day there were many smiles and much laughing. Oh, there were problems at times, but because we liked and trusted each other, troubles were ironed out with little fuss.

Every morning it was a joy to enter the nearly new building, so sun-filled and shiny-clean. Thanks to bus driver / custodian Howard Clark and fellow custodian Adonis Ladner, it was the cleanest schoolhouse I've ever known. Everything was perfect in the morning. Then at noon they closed the boys' room and the girls' room and rewashed the porcelain and the floors.

Several of us had known the old Easton High School on the hill. Once a proud two-story building, it later became a tired place with grimy, oiled floors, mouse-inhabited wicker wastebaskets, and an old furnace that made such noises we were sure it would blow up some cold day. Wayne Dodge and my then husband Don Smith had graduated from the old building, and Wayne had been my student there. Don, Verna Fuller, and I had taught in the old building.

Don had coached basketball there when they had played their games in the low-ceilinged Grange Hall. The room was heated by a woodstove just inches from the playing floor.

I look back and wonder why boys didn't fall onto that hot stove and get badly burned. There was barely room for a row of spectators, whose feet were often on the playing surface. A few more people could sit on the small stage. What a treat to have a beautiful new gymnasium/auditorium with natural wood walls, a high curved ceiling, great lighting, a polished floor, and enough bleacher seating for all the fans. The bleachers were nearly full for games, and the chairs on the floor were filled for all other activities, such as the senior play, the junior exhibition, and concerts. Easton parents and other citizens supported every school event.

In many ways our principal Clair Carter set the tone for our small school. I remember the first time I met him and his wife Eldora; I thought I'd never seen a more handsome young couple. As I got acquainted with them, I learned that they were as good as they looked. Although he was low-key and relaxed, we knew what Clair expected of us. I can't recall ever seeing him angry enough to raise his voice. Since we knew the students from seventh grade through high school, and since we knew their parents and where they lived—many of us had been invited to their homes—there was a warm feeling between Clair, we teachers, the parents, and the kids.

I can remember walking down the long hall from my room to the office. If I heard someone practicing the flute, I would think, "Margaret's getting better all the time." If I heard hammering from the shop, I wondered if John would get that bookcase finished in time for his mother's birthday. One day I glanced into the auditorium and saw music teacher Wendell Tompkins rehearsing a pageant with the first, second, and third graders. Having been brought by bus from the little school, the children were excited to be in such a big space, and wanted to run and run. Wendell, always patient, was saying, "No, Betty, you can't go over there with the buttercups. Run back with the other bluebirds, please."

As I returned to my room I could smell the casserole being prepared by the senior girls. My home economics training had taught me that one must have a cleanup committee for every lab. At Easton High there was never a need for one. Those girls, brought up by rural Aroostook mothers, knew that when you cooked a meal, you washed the dishes and put things away.

I recall that I always had money in my desk drawer—collections for school publications and such—and that I never locked the drawer. I never thought that anyone would take the money. Nobody ever did.

I remember Clair paging me on the intercom and suggesting that I make a pot of coffee for after school. He would say we needed a five-minute teachers' meeting, and that we might be there for a couple of hours. We liked to stay and visit, often sharing what had gone on in our classes. Since we all knew all the kids, it was easy to spot a student who seemed disturbed about something, or who was getting behind in class. We would try to think of ways to help. We had no need for the No Child Left Behind edict that would cause so much trouble at a later time. Sometimes after school we'd have a Ping-Pong tournament going. There was always much teasing and joking.

Every year we put on a supper for the school board members and their spouses. We didn't meet with them to complain about class sizes or to request more pay. We liked them, and we shared their pride in the school. The two members that I remember most fondly are Kendall Bolster, whose wife Olive was a dear friend of mine, and Luman Mahaney, whose wife

Augusta, called Gustie, was a help and an inspiration to me as a young farm wife. I remember one school dance where Gustie appeared beautifully dressed as always, and so sparkling and full of fun. She was one of several Easton women I watched with awe because they could accomplish so much in a day, and do it all with such grace and good nature.

Lib Hoyt was one of my first friends when I moved to Easton as a young wife; we were both bringing up our families on potato farms. At school we often worked together. For instance, we coached girls' basketball. Since Lib had been a good college athlete and I was lacking in athletic ability, I followed her lead. Girls' games were not as important as the boys' games; we played a small schedule, and had no tournaments. We did play Ashland twice every year, though. When we traveled to Ashland they always won the game, and they always put on a supper—a chance for the girls in the two schools to get well acquainted. When they came to Easton they won again, and we put on a supper for them. We had a good time with their coaches and girls, and winning didn't seem that important.

Lib and I also chaperoned cheerleaders to out-of-town games and tournaments in Bangor. Since Bangor was usually warm in March, we found it a treat to leave our snowbanks behind. We stayed with the girls at Cobb's Lodge, an old mansion converted to an inn, and for a while run by former Presque Isle people. One year, however, it was under new management, and conditions were different.

Soon after we arrived we watched a man who appeared to be intoxicated, and who used his key to open all the doors on the second floor, where our rooms were. After that, Lib and I decided to sit up on the balcony outside our rooms, where we could look down at the first floor and desk. Noise increased as the night passed, since there were rooms full of girls from other towns, and many rooms full of boys.

Finally, there was a fight in the lobby—bottles being thrown, much hitting and yelling. Our girls woke up and came out to look over the balcony. One commented that it was just like in the movies, only she couldn't tell the good guys from the bad. Fearing that there were no good guys, we put in a call to the motel where our team and coaches were, saying we were worried for the girls' safety, and asking if one of them could come over for a few hours. When we appealed for help at the desk, we were asked, "Don't you like to see kids having fun?" We didn't fare any better with our own men, who said we'd be fine.

To be sure, we all survived the long night. At one point a girl somewhere was calling, "Help! Oh, help!" Lib and I decided we had to go to the girl's aid. When we knocked on the door a big, rugged girl opened it and said, "Why don't you mind your own business?" So much for trying to save a damsel from a fate worse than death!

I pause on the page of the yearbook picturing dear Verna Fuller. When I was a young teacher she had already worked hard to bring up a big family. I often relied on her calmness, kindness, and wisdom, and frequently asked her for advice. Several of her children were in my classes in the old building.

Jim and Nonie Ugone came to Easton when they were young, much like Clair and Eldora Carter. They were also well loved. In later years Jim became a much-respected principal at Caribou High School. In retirement they have a home in Fort Fairfield, and winter in Florida.

Every spring we all accompanied the seniors—there were eighteen in the class of 1959—to York's in New Brunswick, for a banquet. I think Clair must have jotted down some notes through the years, for he always had a good supply of funny and slightly embarrassing stories about each student. Since he told nothing hurtful, the kids waited eagerly to see what Mr. Carter would say about them and their classmates in his after-dinner speech.

Although we offered few extracurricular activities, each student had a wide variety of experiences. All the juniors took part in junior declamations; all the seniors were in the senior play. A high percentage of the boys were on the basketball and baseball teams, and most of the kids belonged to Future Homemakers and Future Farmers organizations. Everyone worked on class and school moneymaking campaigns. We were all in it together.

Although the school was small, students could learn to trust themselves and to think for themselves. Earlier in the 1950s, student Gloria Hagernan found a mistake in a home economics textbook. There was a statement that one formation of kitchen appliances was more efficient than another certain formation. Gloria doubted the statement, so we tested many pretend-cooking experiences in each setting. Gloria proved to be right, so I sent all our documentation to the head of the state home economics department. She sent the information to the publishers. They corrected their book and sent a check for a fairly large sum to the head of the department. Later I wished that we had sent our material directly to the publisher so that Gloria might have received the money, but we were trained back then to go through the proper channels. Perhaps the publisher would have ignored a letter from a small high school, anyway.

Back then we home economics teachers had great leeway in course planning. I developed what the state department called the first such class in Maine: a family living course for senior boys and girls. The students chose a salary typical for young people at the time, and they researched the cost of rent, insurance, and car maintenance. They planned meals and found costs of the foods used. There was much joking, with girls describing the handsome hunks they would marry and the wonderful meals they would cook for them. Yet both boys and girls were surprised to find out how much it cost to run a household. As the weeks passed, I was amused to hear one girl say, "You know what my husband will be like? Little skinny guy with not much of an appetite."

Many of the warm and wonderful attributes of small schools are immeasurable. Sometimes at Easton High School we seemed more like a big family than a dignified educational institution. Although we respected Clair as an excellent principal, I'm afraid we sometimes treated him more like a friend or a relative than a boss. He told me recently, for instance, that Lib often scolded him for not cleaning his glasses. She would go into his office, take his glasses off his face, clean them, and hand them back to him.

Howard and Adonis, the custodians, were also part of the family. Once, without meaning to, I gave Howard a scare. A merchant in Mars Hill called and told me he was discarding a female mannequin, and asked if I'd like to have her for the home economics room. I said yes, knowing that my girls would find it fun to choose outfits for her. On a Sunday Don and I went to get her, and stopped to leave her off at the schoolhouse. Because she was nude I didn't put her up on her stand. Instead, I stretched her out behind the divan, planning to bring in something on Monday morning to drape over her until the girls could dress her.

Howard went in earlier than I did, and said he nearly fainted when in the early-morning shadows he saw a nude woman on the floor. Don told Howard that he wished he had thought to add fake blood and a knife to really give him a scare.

Both Howard and Adonis were great jokers. Once, on a bus trip, taking a group of girls to a convention in Augusta, a friend, Wilda Wathen, went along to chaperone. Wilda had two sons who had been my students, and she was always willing to help out at school. On the way home the two of us were having a good visit in the seat behind Adonis. The girls had curled up with their pillows and gone to sleep. Then Adonis gave his little laugh, saying, "All the chickens are sleeping. I wonder when the old hens will go to roost?" From some people that would have been an insulting remark, but from dear Adonis, it was just funny, and we all laughed.

I keep staring at the faculty picture, hating to leave those days. I am saddened that Wayne, Verna, Don, and Lib are no longer living, happy that Clair and Eldora are enjoying retirement in their Easton home. I've lost track of Bob Beek and Allen Smallidge, yet there we all are, frozen in time.

I think about Don. Our farm was closer to Easton, yet it was legally in Presque Isle, so our sons went to school there. Still, they had ties to Easton, because when they were in the lower grades, Don would often open the gym on a Saturday morning or afternoon so the Easton kids could go in and play basketball. Of course, our boys went along.

One day one of them brought a visiting friend from Presque Isle. It was probably Steve, since Barney and Mel were very young at the time. Later the mother of our young visitor told me that her son came home and said, "Steve's parents must be awful rich—his dad owns a gym!"

None of us had much money back then, yet in my years at Easton High School, I was in many ways "awful rich."

# 6

# Carefully Taught

A SONG IN THE MUSICAL *South Pacific* proclaims that we are not born with our prejudices, but that "We have to be carefully taught." I was taught by my village and some relatives that only Protestants can go to Heaven, and not all of them make it. Because ministers for our little church were supplied by a Methodist seminary, it was obvious that Methodists made it past the pearly gates—but only if they behaved themselves on this Earth. All good people were white and Protestant; they were also Republicans.

We saw people of other colors who were servants for summer people, and even though most of us in the village worked for summer people, we felt superior to the black and Asian servants. The one Native American in our town, Mr. Jeremy, was a talented wood-carver, but we did not see him as our equal. Once my grandmother told me that I should not play with one of the boys in my school "because his great-grandmother was a full-blooded Indian, and if you married him, you might have a papoose."

At some point in my growing up I wanted to respect the rights of all people, but I had much early teaching to overcome. Yet years later, when it seemed to me that most of us were rid of our prejudices, little islands of fear and hatred would surface. I was surprised when my father, a well-read and thoughtful man, was furious because the seminary had supplied a black minister on the Sunday when the Masonic Lodge marched to church in a body.

There were many examples of religious prejudices. One day in my first teaching job in 1941, I saw two seventh-grade boys fighting on the playground. I asked what the problem was. Each maintained that he had the only real religion, and the proof they offered was that in one church, wine was used for Communion, and in the other, grape juice.

"It says wine in the Bible," the Catholic boy stated.

"Drinking alcohol is a sin," the Protestant replied.

They asked me to decide the matter, and I told the Catholic to ask his priest, the Protestant to ask his minister. I hope I encouraged them to be friends and to respect each other's differences.

I had a Catholic girl student who married a Protestant boy, and I was sad that both their families practically disowned their children. The girl's mother refused to attend either the bridal shower or her daughter's wedding.

When I moved to Aroostook I heard that many years ago, there had been an active Ku Klux Klan group in Presque Isle. Since there were few blacks for them to harass, they burned crosses for people of French heritage. One year I held University of Maine evening extension classes in Madawaska. The class was called "Communication," but when I met the members, fifteen to twenty bright, likable young women, I learned that they wanted me to help them erase all traces of their French accent. They could speak French, but they intended to forget it and move away from the area as soon as possible. Some of them had been punished by teachers who had caught them speaking French on the playground; many had been mistreated by boys and men who considered French girls "easy."

I was shocked. I told them how often I wished I could speak two languages. Sometimes when skiing at Mont Farlagne, I'd have coffee in the lodge with women who would ask if I spoke French. When I said no, they would speak English. Although they treated me kindly, I felt ignorant and inferior.

I had tried to learn French in high school where reading the language was stressed, and I had taken night school courses to learn to converse, but I had nobody with whom to practice, and I retained little. When I was a chaperone on a Presque Isle High School French Club trip to Paris, I had to rely on a student to help me order food or purchase simple items. Kerry Munson, who had learned French in school and at home, was my interpreter.

I doubt that I influenced many of the women in my extension class, since for their lifetimes they had been taught that being French was inferior. There have been changes, however. Many schools now start French in lower grades, and students learn French history and culture along with the language. In my youth I remember hearing about Lafayette, but I learned little else about France. In postcollege courses I learned to value French culture as I studied the art and literature of France.

On my mother's side I had a French ancestor named LaSalle. I am sorry that later the name was Americanized to Lassell. I like to imagine that I owe some of my love of life to an ancient LaSalle, since my English and Swedish forebears did little smiling in their pictures.

At times I have been discriminated against because I am female. In college, when I expressed the wish to major in biology and become a researcher, I was told that since I was a girl,

I should plan on getting a more suitable job wherever my husband wanted to live.

Years later, one morning when I had to get to school early for a department meeting, I stopped for gas. There was nobody ahead of me, so I hoped I would make it on time. Then a truck drove up and the attendant, who was about to pump my gas, changed his mind and filled both big tanks on the truck. When I asked him why he did that, he said, "Why, Glenna, he's a man, and he has to get to work."

Students and faculty loved Franklin Cunningham, my first principal at Presque Isle High School, yet he was a man of his time. Since I directed plays and held evening rehearsals, I requested a key to the building, but Mr. Cunningham said, "No, no. Use Don's key." When I explained that Don was often out of town for ball games on nights when I had rehearsals, Mr. Cunningham told me to go then to Jim Dyer's house and borrow his key. Finally, assistant principal Clarence Keegan persuaded Mr. Cunningham that I needed my own key. Women teachers could be entrusted with the education of the youth of Presque Isle, but were not trustworthy enough to have their own keys to the school.

Yet through it all, I felt sure I had conquered all my prejudices. Then one summer I received a grant to attend San Jose State College of California. I lived in a high-rise dormitory where my institute occupied one floor. Another floor housed black high school students, there for an Upward Bound summer, and there was another floor of white students, taking a similar course. I realized that when I rode up on an elevator filled with white kids, I would notice this girl's smile, that boy's freckles; yet when I rode up in an elevator filled with black kids, who were equally friendly, I would think of them as those nice black kids. I didn't see them as individuals. I was as bad as Archie Bunker, who said they all looked alike.

An incident back in the 1950s still horrifies me. One night during a blizzard a young Southern man who lived in an apartment we rented told me that the road was blocked and a car was stuck in front of our house. I asked if there were people in the car, and when he said yes, I asked him to bring them in. He said he couldn't do that because they were niggers. I said, "Then I will go out for them."

When he realized that I was angry with him, he went out and brought back a young couple with two babies, probably ages two and one. I couldn't believe that they would sit out there on a freezing cold night rather than come to our door. The couple seemed very shy, and they were all cold. I produced hot food and threw a log in the fireplace. Then in the hubbub of babies crying and me rushing around, my young sons woke up and came padding down the stairs. Since I didn't think they had ever seen black children, I wondered what they would say. Little Barney said to me, "Oh, Mommy, aren't they cute?" No mention of color. I guess it's true that you have to be carefully taught.

Through the years I have also encountered religious prejudice. On another night a few years later, when the road beyond our house was again blocked by a snowstorm, a man got stuck in front of our house. He came to the door, we invited him in, and since we were about to eat supper, we invited him to join us. He asked if we were going to say grace. We said no, that was not our custom. He asked if he could say one, and we said yes. He talked for several minutes while the food was getting cold. He thanked God for sending him to a household that needed soul-saving. He promised he would do his best to lead us to the fold, and on and on.

After supper, Don climbed onto his tractor in the biting cold and pulled the man in his car up the hill and down the other side to where he lived, at least a half-mile away. Again the man thanked God, but didn't thank Don for getting him home, and didn't thank us for supper.

When Don returned, shivering, Steve said, "Daddy, if he gets stuck here again, can we leave him in his car?"

I have observed through the years that my sons and my grandchildren have fewer prejudices than I inherited. There are many little islands of hope among young people today— many examples that they are being carefully taught to respect the differences of all people.

# 7

# The School Bus

I FIRST RODE A SCHOOL BUS in the early 1930s, when I finished primary school in Ashville and moved on to grammar school in North Sullivan. Our bus was a big yellow metal box on wheels. The seats were uncomfortable and we had a freezing cold ride. I last rode a bus in 1990, my final year of teaching at Presque Isle High School. That bus was a yellow metal box on wheels with uncomfortable seats. Although heaters had been invented, they behaved so erratically that the students at the back might be begging the driver to turn up the heat while those in the middle were complaining of being so hot they could die. If cars had improved through the years at the same rate as school buses, we'd barely be out of the age of the Model T.

The people who thought up school buses had to hate kids, or they would have made some of the seats comfortable for somebody. The seats were too high for little kids, and the distance between was too narrow for high school students. Both seats and backs were so hard that on long trips, even those of us who were well padded had a hard time getting comfortable. Then, too, if the designers had liked kids, they would have installed seat belts, so little children wouldn't be flung against metal walls in case of an accident.

Yet despite my complaints, in many weeks during my teaching years I spent more hours on buses than I spent at home.

45

When I taught at Easton High School, and later, at Fort Fairfield High School, I chaperoned home economics students to Future Homemakers conventions in Augusta. Then at Presque Isle High School, in all the years that I was cheerleader advisor, I rode on the team bus to all out-of-town games and tournaments. In fact, I was hired at PIHS because the principal did not have a woman teacher who would ride buses with cheerleaders, and since my sons were basketball players, he assumed that I wouldn't mind riding on the team bus.

Since I also worked with the high school theater program, I rode buses to all our regional, state, and New England drama competitions. Then, in months when there was neither basketball nor a play contest, I might chaperone a French Club trip to Quebec, a biology field trip to the Maine coast, or a government class trip to Augusta. One year we took the high school band to exchange concerts in Nova Scotia. Since we in the County are hundreds of miles from everywhere, many of our trips were long ones, and often included overnight stays.

So why did I do all that if I hated buses so much? I willingly rode the team bus because I would have gone to my sons' games anyway. And all the others? I liked the kids, I liked chaperoning with my colleagues, and, in spite of the hard seats, I always enjoyed myself.

I sometimes got tired of eating fast food, but with a big crew and tight schedules, we couldn't stop at restaurants. McDonald's did a smart thing when they opted to give bus drivers free meals. Sometimes our kids would request another fast-food drive-through, but somehow the bus always drove into McDonald's.

I do admire bus drivers, though. Not only are they skilled drivers who take on an awesome responsibility daily, but they also have to deal with noise, with kids who are slow to get on and off the bus, with fights and tears, with kids who don't want to sit in their seats—the list goes on. Bus drivers never know what will happen next.

I smile when I recall a trip with Presque Isle cheerleaders who were to attend an all-day workshop somewhere south of Bangor. To arrive in time for the opening meeting, we needed to leave Presque Isle at four in the morning. Sleepy parents brought their sleepy daughters to the bus, the girls carrying pillows and blankets and hoping for another nap. Only one girl, a lovable little blonde named Louise, seemed to be wide awake. She climbed on the bus a few minutes before departure time and stopped beside the bus driver, a dignified and somewhat shy older man. He looked up and asked her if she needed something. Louise gave him a big smile. She said, "I'm trying to decide if I should go into the schoolhouse and pee one more time. If I don't, I may have to go someplace where we can't stop. But if I go, I may get in the habit and then have to go again . . ."

I was sitting where I could see the side of the driver's face. I feared he might faint from embarrassment. I think he was the same man who sometimes got nervous in city traffic. Once he got on the rotary in Augusta and kept going around and around, despite advice about exits from the coach.

Like the students, I also tried to sleep on long bus trips. It is possible to sleep on a school bus, but it takes practice. If you put your pillow on the window side you can curl your feet up, but the vibration may give you a headache. If you put it behind your back, you have no place to put your feet. If the bus isn't full and you have a whole seat to yourself, you are tempted to stretch your legs out into the aisle, but then surely a student back there somewhere will wake up and decide to bring wrappings and pop bottles to the trash can beside the driver. Then there will surely be a little bump in the road and the student will run into your feet, drop the trash, and cause everyone to wake up. Even under the best of napping conditions, you will awake with a stiff neck and a back that is all out of kilter.

On another dark, early-morning trip, most of the students were sleeping when we left Houlton for I-95. Then as the sun came up, a boy said, "Look! There's a deer!" Others sat up and looked out. "There's another one!" "There are three more!" We counted eight beautiful creatures in the mist—one of the many good moments on bus rides.

We couldn't choose our drivers, but on our drama competition trips, we loved having Mae assigned to us. She could drive skillfully under all conditions, she enjoyed the kids, and she liked going to the competitions with us. It was great having a bus and driver handy in case of emergencies.

However, there was one New England trip that tested her abilities. We were staying on a college campus with narrow streets and no provisions for bus parking, so Mae spent the weekend maneuvering us out of tight places. Once, when she was carefully getting us out of such a spot, a group of loud and cocky local boys jumped up on the bus and told her they could move the vehicle if she would do as they said. She got off the bus and with tone and words that left no doubt in their minds, told them where they should go, when they should go there, and what the consequences would be if they didn't comply.

Realizing they weren't dealing with a scared little woman from up there in the sticks of Maine, they quickly ran away, and our kids cheered for Mae.

On long bus trips, kids passed the time visiting with friends, reading, playing games, and singing. Also, on drama competition trips we had coloring contests. We had a big collection of coloring books and crayons, the only rule being that the coloring must be done on a moving bus. We saved the finished pages, displayed them on the walls at our spring banquet, had judges choose winners, and gave gag prizes.

When we saw richer schools arriving at contests in fancy charter buses, we were envious. But if some of our kids had fallen in love with kids from other schools and wanted to talk about the romance, or if they'd had a great time watching all those other plays, or if they sang on the way home until they were too sleepy to sing another note, and if perchance we had won something, we were just as happy in our big yellow metal box as we would've been in more-elegant transportation.

# 8

# At My Worst

BY THE TIME I WAS TEN I had been twice consumed by
that monster emotion, jealousy. Both times another woman
had stolen a man I considered my own.

Once a year my uncle Henry drove his snappy Chrysler
roadster to East Sullivan to visit his family. He was my hero
because he would talk to me, because he wore classy clothes,
and because he would take me for rides in his wonderful car.
That coupe would go twenty-five miles an hour on our rutted
dirt roads. For weeks I looked forward to Uncle Henry's visits,
and I missed him when he went back to Boston.

Then one summer when he drove in and I rushed out to
meet him, there, sitting in the car with my very own uncle,
was a wife. No one had told me about her. I hated that grinning woman on sight. Everyone, and especially Uncle Henry,
made a fuss over Aunt Bessie. I was ordered to hug Aunt Bessie, to kiss Aunt Bessie. I didn't want to be in the room with
Aunt Bessie. I wanted Aunt Bessie dead. I was never once
invited to ride in the car. I daydreamed about what I could do
and say to that horrible woman, but my fear of spankings from
Papa kept me from being rude. I was glad when the two of
them headed back to Boston. I became fond of Aunt Bessie in
later years, but it took time.

Next I see myself in Ashville Elementary School. I may have
been ten at the time, for that schoolhouse was built when I

was nine. I have spotty memories of my schoolmates there and my relationships with them. I recall that many of the kids disliked me, and no wonder.

An only child, I had no understanding of other kids' feelings. I'm ashamed to say that I was an obnoxious show-off. If I received a good grade I bragged about it loudly, despite Mama's attempts to make me meek and ladylike.

Back then at recess and noon hour, the only thing we did was run around the schoolhouse. Although that seems strange now, at the time it was the thing to do. We weren't racing; we just ran and ran, one behind the other. When some of us grew tired we stopped for a few minutes and watched the other runners. I often watched Ralph Robertson, who, along with his sister Faustina, was in my class. One day I told Faustina that I liked Ralph. The next day she told me that Ralph liked me too. Thus he became my boyfriend.

I can't remember ever talking to Ralph, but I spent more and more time staring at him running around the schoolhouse. I think we wrote a few notes to each other, but I can't imagine what we said in them. We couldn't have written many words, for we wadded those bits of paper up into tiny balls. Some daring kids threw their notes onto other kids' desks even during school. I didn't do that until I was in seventh grade at North Sullivan Grammar School. At that time Mr. Fickett intercepted and read aloud to the whole school my note to Arno, the boy of my dreams at the time. I wished for death, sure that there could be nothing good in my life after that.

My notes to Ralph, however, went safely home with Faustina, and his to me came back by the same route. I knew this was true love, and that I would grow up to marry Ralph and have lots of kids. Although the notes were our only communication, I continued to watch him running around the schoolhouse, and sometimes when I sensed that he was watching me run, I would lengthen my stride, flail my arms, and go like the wind.

I had one big problem at the time, however. When some of the boys were watching and I was running, they started calling me a horrible name. "Birdie Johnson! Birdie, Birdie, Birdie!" They would point at me and jeer. I don't know why I considered that name so horrible, but I would scream at them and threaten to tell my father. I assured them that he would beat up their fathers, which of course spurred them on to worse taunting. They pointed out the ways in which their fathers were superior to my father. The most important way—the superior length of a certain part of their fathers' bodies.

Although I hated and feared those boys, I was happy that Ralph would be my boyfriend forever.

Then one day Faustina told me that I should not write any more notes to Ralph. When I asked her why not, she told me that he no longer liked me—that he now liked Corris. Corris—who didn't even run around the schoolhouse. She just sat around looking sweet and demure. How could Ralph want a girl like that?

Corris had been my friend and playmate since we were little. We lived in castles on the ledges and sailed ships in the millstream. I didn't even resent her all the times Mama said, "Why can't you be like Corris?" I remember Mama pointing to our school picture and saying, "Look at Corris." There she sat, her dress as clean as when she'd left home in the morning, her bangs neat, her knees together, her hands folded in her lap.

Then Mama sighed. "Look at you," she said. My legs were sprawled apart, my dress wadded up between them in a most unladylike fashion, my knees scratched and bloody, and my hair, which started the morning with curls and a hair ribbon, now tousled and windblown. The hair ribbon may have stuck in the tree I climbed.

I didn't blame Corris for Mama's comparisons. Yet now that she had stolen the man I was supposed to spend my life with, I hated her with more venom than I had known existed. She had taken the only one I could ever love. They would marry and live happily ever after and have all the beautiful babies I was supposed to have. I would be a pitiful old maid, and people would point at me and whisper, "Poor old Birdie, Birdie, Birdie." My heart was broken. The tortures I'd wished on Aunt Bessie were nothing compared to the fates I dreamed up for Corris.

This time I took action. I wrote a note to Corris, wadded it up into a little ball, and on my way home from school, I threw it on her lawn. I didn't sign my name, so nobody would know who wrote it. In it I must have called her some bad names. Still, I don't think I knew any really horrible words back then. Anyway, her mother saw what I did, and after I passed by she must have gone out to retrieve the note. Then on the next Sunday morning she brought it to church and handed it to my father. "Glenna wrote this," she said.

The spanking with his leather slipper was a really bad one. For a while my rear end hurt almost as much as my broken heart did. The result of this experience: I had written the first and the last hate letter of my lifetime. Corris grew up and married Clive, and I lost track of Ralph. Yet in my short relationship with him, I learned all I needed to know about the awful power of the destructive emotion we call jealousy.

# 9

# Say When

SAY WHEN SUGGESTS A LEVEL OF CONTROL, of moderation. Yet often when we reach a perfect level, we still feel we must push ahead another notch or two.

Take dogs. Everyone my age—north of ninety—remembers when most dogs worked for a living. They brought the cows in from the pasture, kept the pigs in the pen, guarded the children on their way to school. They ate table scraps, and were never taken to a vet. If they became sick or injured, they were shot, and the farmer got another dog.

When I was a young wife our border collie, Cheeta, was so loyal to our baby that when my mother visited and took little Steve for a ride in his carriage, Cheeta wouldn't allow her to leave our lawn. As Mama was about to enter the road, Cheeta put his mouth around her ankle and wouldn't let go until Mama turned around and came back to the house.

Gradually time produced fewer farms, more urban dwellers, and the working dog became the family pet—man's, woman's, and kids' best friend. This dog was given proper nutrition, preventive shots, and loving care. That was a good place to be, for family and dog.

But did we stop there? Some of us had to push on—to breed dogs for competitions, of all things. I don't know who decided on the ideal for each breed, but soon dog fanciers scrambled to own a dog with the perfect leg length, coat sheen, and shape of ears. Dogs were groomed and trained for shows, often at great expense.

Dog shows are great spectacles—huge crowds in the stands, many owners rooting for their dogs—the floor of the huge arena filled with dogs of every imaginable breed being fussed over by groomers. And there are the handlers, often young women looking oh so serious, and dressed in suits with skirts so tight around the hem that I don't see how they can run. Often they dress in colors that show off the dogs to best advantage. A handler may be all in black as she shows a white Samoyed. Around and around the ring she runs, the would-be champion on a short leash. She holds the head to best advantage and adjusts her gait to the dog's best speed.

I love looking at the dogs—at the amazing lengths breeders have reached to improve, or at least change, the original dog who was everybody's best friend. Yet sometimes it is even more fun to see the humans who have been bred to run the show. The judge is by far the grandest and most important person there. He may be a portly, white-haired gentleman in a tuxedo, or she may be a tall, queenly lady in a long black velvet gown. Observing her manner, one sees that her job is of world-shaking importance. She strides around, watching, asking for re-runs, running her hands over every part of each dog's body, and finally making the vitally important decision that will bring a measure of fame to one owner and heartbreak to many others.

In a recent televised show I stared at the Samoyed with the long white hair and the curled-up bushy tail. I was amazed to see that he looked exactly like my dog Buddy, my best friend in the 1920s. Yet Buddy was no prize dog. His mother was not nearly as beautiful as he was, having spots of brown mixed with her white coat, and a tail that didn't curl up much. Buddy was given to us by a neighbor. I doubt anyone knew who the father was, since all dogs ran free back then. Yet somehow Buddy looked like a champion. Nature seemed to do some interesting breeding without human help.

Then I stare at the Pekingese and remember summer people carrying these little dogs around. I never thought they were worthy to be called dogs; such ugly little black faces and vacant eyes, and with their extremely long fur, I never knew for sure whether they had legs. My view of them has never changed. I watch the current representative of the breed, who is not much different from the earlier model. I see a dust mop that is somehow being propelled around the floor. Before his last showing his beautician arranges every hair.

Then there are all the best-of-breed prizes—such beautiful terriers, St. Bernards, Irish setters. There is riotous applause. Proud owners are aglow.

And then the hushed silence, the suspense; which of these champions will be Best of Show? The queen in black velvet takes her time, asks each to parade around again. She milks her moment. And then—oh, no! She chooses the Pekingese— the ambulatory mop. How could she, from all those wonderful creatures who actually look like dogs? I fear I am seeing civilization getting just too precious. Way back there, someone should have said when.

# Part Two:

# Getting Married

# 10

# This Is the Way

IN FIRST GRADE WE SANG A SONG, "This Is the Way to Start a New Day." As I sit here eating an orange, I realize that breakfast has always been a favorite part of my day.

I have an early memory of lying in my little upstairs bedroom over the post office and, through the iron-grate floor register, smelling bacon cooking. I would pull on my slippers and the bathrobe Mama made and trudge downstairs to the shed-kitchen behind the post office. There was no bathroom. I'd wash my face and hands in the washbasin in the sink. Then I'd eat an orange, a bowl of oatmeal with cream and berries on it, or a banana in winter, and one of Mama's fluffy biscuits with butter and wild strawberry jam, along with a glass of milk.

Finally I had to forego Mama's breakfast for those at college. I remember waiting on tables, having to eat with the busboys and other waitresses before we served the dorm members. Cheffie Fitch gave us all the seconds we wanted. He made great French toast and scrambled eggs.

In early years on the farm I loved cooking breakfast for a hungry husband and three hungry sons. I was grateful that they all woke up good-natured early in the morning. Sometimes the boys invented crazy games at the table. I fear that we sometimes substituted fun for perfect etiquette.

I had a grill that covered two burners on the gas stove, so I could cook large amounts of French toast or pancakes, ham, or bacon and eggs in a short time. There was always orange juice and milk, and often homemade chocolate doughnuts. I shudder to think of the fat and sugar in these breakfasts, yet my family burned up all those calories in their long and active days.

In my years of living alone I find it easy to grab something quick rather than something more nutritious and tasty. Lunch may be a sandwich; supper may be warmed over from the last two nights.

But then there is breakfast. After my orange, I cook oatmeal (never the sugary kind in the packets), and add banana, blueberries, and vanilla soy milk. Then there's my one cup of coffee, which I adore. One reason for loving breakfast: I eat it in the morning, when my rural world is new and clean, and when I have been given the gift of another day.

I'm glad I was born into an age where mamas got up early, built the fire, and slow-cooked the oatmeal in a double boiler. Now the world has changed—and only sometimes for the better. Many of us have given up some of the fat and sugars in those early farm spreads, yet when I watch some ads on TV, I want to cry. There are the children trying to feed the hated oatmeal to the dog while the announcer points out that good mommies give their families what they love—frosted Pop-Tarts. Then Jimmy Dean sneers at cereal, suggesting a greasy sausage sandwich on white bread as the perfect breakfast.

Today many women don't have the luxury of time to cook a leisurely breakfast; they have to be out the door along with husband and children, dressed and groomed for work. Gone are the long, happy conversations, the bright dishes on red-checked tablecloths. Yet it doesn't take long to drink a glass of orange juice, or eat a slice of whole-wheat toast with peanut butter. If there are a few minutes for sitting down, there are nutritious dry cereals—and bananas are quick to eat.

In my teaching years I watched many kids go, at recess, to a convenience store for breakfast—a bottle of Coke and a couple of candy bars. After the quick sugar fix wore off, they were lethargic again.

I have young relatives whose idea of breakfast is a cup of coffee or cappuccino from a drive-through on their way to work. I tell myself they'll be okay; they'll still drive safely, and they'll eat a healthy meal later in the day.

I'm still enjoying life at north of ninety, and feel that I must give at least some of the credit to eating a good breakfast each day.

# 11

# Just a Girl

IN MY LIFETIME I've watched the ways women view themselves and the ways they are viewed by society. I learned at a young age by hiding behind counters in the former dry goods store where my mother ran the Ashville Post Office. There I listened to women who came early for their mail.

Typical conversations included:

"It looks like rain. Do you think the clothes will dry on the line?"

"John says they will. John says it won't rain until night."

"You folks going to Bar Harbor for the Fourth of July?"

"Don't know. Peter hasn't said yet."

Both women and men assumed that men were superior and in charge, and since the men in the village were mostly good people who did well by their wives and children, there were few complaints.

Only in the presence of women did I hear complaints about men:

"He hates to cut his toenails, and that makes me mad. I'm always darning his socks."

"He says he doesn't have time to take his boots off every time he comes into the house. I spend half my time on my hands and knees, scrubbing the kitchen floor."

At our house Mama and I were not allowed to look at the Bangor paper until Papa had finished with it. He said, "A man has a right to a paper that isn't all messed up." In the evening while men were reading their virgin papers, the women were darning, mending, or knitting.

One woman in our village sometimes argued loudly with her husband. Other women did not see her as a champion of their rights, however. They said, "Who does she think she is? Is she trying to wear the pants in the family? Poor Sam, having to put up with her."

I was an only child, but my uncle Justin and aunt Ethel had four sons. Papa often told people that his nephews were much smarter than I was. He had a favorite story: "My grandfather weighed 300 pounds, my father weighed 200 pounds, I weigh 100 pounds, and I don't even have a son." When he told it, everyone laughed but me.

Women seemed to want their first child to be a boy. Today a girl is often her daddy's little princess, but I never attained that status. The first play clothes I remember were khaki jodhpurs, jacket, and army hat. I carried a toy rifle. Papa bought me a little wheelbarrow so I could help wheel in the wood. I still have my little saw. Despite the long curls and Mama's hair ribbons, I grew up trying to be a boy. Although Mama never said anything in front of Papa, she let me know that she didn't like my noisy bragging and showing off.

She had a favorite quotation: "Be good, sweet maid, and let who will be clever." I understood that being "good" meant being meek, quiet, and obedient.

Yet feeling that I was an inferior girl and that Mama was an inferior woman persisted. One day I called home from high school to ask permission to stay after school to watch a baseball game. Mama said, "I can't say, dear, and your father isn't here right now."

Boys' basketball was a popular spectator sport, but girls' basketball was a joke, and the most boring game imaginable. We couldn't dribble the ball, but one bounce was allowed. We couldn't run because there were three courts, and no girl could go out of her court. In the center court were two centers and two side-centers who could do nothing but catch the ball and pass it to the other courts, which contained two forwards and two guards. Only forwards could shoot. This meant that most of the players were standing around much of the time. There was a later change to two courts, which was only slightly better.

When we girls asked why we couldn't play by boys' rules, we were given stock answers:

"Girls aren't strong enough for all that running."

"Girls are emotional, and they cry easily under stress."

"If girls developed their muscles, they might not have babies easily."

Recently at an athletic Hall of Fame ceremony I saw Kim Condon receive an award. Kim, a tall and lovely young woman, was one of the stars on a Presque Isle High School championship team. I told her I wished the people expressing the "wisdom" of my youth could have seen her team in action. How amazed they would have been.

In college I was still "just a girl." My unstated reason for going to college was supposed to be to catch a husband. At the University of Maine in the 1930s, the ratio was about one girl to seven men, so the odds were on the side of us husband-hunters. In my early years, however, I wanted to major in science and be a researcher. I loved lab work in bacteriology, and my grades were good; however, I was told, "You're just a girl, and you must be a nurse, secretary, or teacher. Then you can get a job wherever your husband wants to settle."

I continued to be pushed into home economics because at that time, home ec and agriculture teachers were federally funded. They often received higher salaries than principals—a big incentive. This situation was no longer true when I graduated, and I had little respect for most of my home ec classes. Perhaps I fed my family better because of my nutritional courses; for instance, I learned how to pasteurize milk and how to can foods safely. I also learned about vitamins and minerals. Yet come to think of it, my mother produced delicious and healthful meals with little or no concern for vitamins.

I liked some of the clothing courses, but I had learned how to sew from Mama and Gram Johnson, and most of the other courses seemed a waste of time. There was great emphasis on dating, for instance. I can't recall learning anything about sex or real values, although much was made about how to catch a man. We were told, "Don't beat a boy at a game. Find out what his interests are so you can ask intelligent questions. Don't talk about yourself. Make yourself as alluring as possible with your hairdo, makeup, and clothes, but still look demure and ladylike."

Even our dorm matron, Mrs. McGinley, gave dating advice. In a dorm session she told us not to kiss on the first date. One girl asked, "How about the second date?" The answer, "Better not. You might be considered easy." My pretty roommate June said, "If I don't give a boy a good-night kiss, he'll think I don't like him, and he won't ask for another date." Mrs. McGinley said, "Here's what you do: You give a little laugh and say sweetly, 'Not now.' Then he knows there's hope for him in the future."

We girls found that advice so hilarious that on the next Friday night when we returned to the dorm at 10:25 (for our 10:30 p.m. curfew), we said to our dates when they bent down for a kiss, "Ha ha—not now." The boys thought that was funny, too.

We were taught that we should never open a car door. If we were double-dating and getting into the backseat, we must never slide over. The boy must walk around the car and get in the other door. I applaud good manners when they show kindness and thoughtfulness, but the "sliding over" rule seemed silly to us young, able-bodied girls.

In "marriage" classes, subterfuge was often recommended. One teacher said, "If you put a dent in the family car, don't tell your husband until you have cooked and served his favorite meal. Be sure you are wearing perfume and an alluring outfit. When he has finished his cream pie, pout and say, 'Honey, I put the teensy-weensiest little dent in a fender today.'" More evidence that the man is the master, the woman the slave. If the slave is clever, perhaps she can use sex to her advantage and avoid punishment.

Since the term *old maid* implied a bad state, there was great emphasis on marrying right out of college. Although many of us married for love, some of us married to avoid being single. In my senior dorm, several of us had been given diamonds by our boyfriends, who had graduated the year before. Sometimes we would meet in the bathroom on a Saturday night and have a "sparkle party," which involved polishing our proof that we had each caught our man. Is that pathetic, or what!

Like my father, my husband had his favorite story:

A father is speaking to his son on the boy's wedding day. "Establish right away that you are in charge. Take her on a buggy ride with a balky horse. The first time the horse stops, say, 'That's once.' The second time, say, 'That's twice.' On the third time, get out of the buggy and shoot the horse. Then the first time your wife displeases you, say, 'That's once.' Things will go your way from that time on."

I didn't laugh at that story either.

The years went by, and I enjoyed farm life, teaching school, and, most of all, watching my boys grow up. Yet now and then I was reminded of a woman's place in the big scheme. One morning in my first summer on the farm, Don asked me if I'd come out and drive the horses in the hay field, since the young man who worked for him was down with a flu bug. I was happy to be out in the sunshine, working with Don. The horses, however, didn't know me, and acted skittish. Although my stops and starts were a bit jerky, I knew I could improve.

Nevertheless, after a few minutes the old hired man said to Don, "The gee-hossley hay field is no place for a gee-hossley woman. Either she goes or I go." I held my breath. Don said, "You'd better go to the house, Glenna." And to the hired man he said, "I'll go over and get one of Jake's boys."

I returned to the house with the sad knowledge that keeping the hired man happy was more important than keeping the wife happy.

There have been some good changes along the way. As I observe young women who are the ages of my granddaughters, I see more good friendships, more equality in relationships. Many of us have learned that a good relationship is the best thing that life has to offer, but that living alone is better than a bad relationship.

Still, people sympathize with me that I haven't "found another husband." When I am asked why, I say that whole days go by when there is no line of men outside my door, asking for my hand in marriage.

And there is another reason: With my earlier conditioning, I fear that if I had remarried and my husband had said "Jump!," I would have asked, "Is this high enough, dear?"

# 12

# Spring Cleaning

WHEN EDNA JACOBS SAID, "I guess I'll clean the sitting room tomorrow," her family groaned, knowing what lay ahead. Tom and the boys would have to get up before their usual time, four o'clock, and carry water for the big copper boiler on the cookstove, fill the stove tank, fill the rinse tub and all the pails. Then they would move the contents of the room—couch, rocking chairs, Morris chair, stands, desk, bookcase—out onto the veranda or into the dooryard. They would hang the big wool rug on the clothesline, where the younger children would beat it with brooms. When the boys would start a broom fight, Edna would come out and set them straight. When only the black iron sitting-room stove was left, a boy would shovel out the ashes. The girls would put on stove black and then polish it until it met Edna's standards.

Edna herself would climb the stepladder and scrub the ceiling. If it still looked gray from the stove and lamp smoke, one of the boys would give it a coat of whitewash. The women, meanwhile, would remove the cretonne couch cover, the pillow covers, the Morris chair covers, and the curtains. They would start the wash, which couldn't be hung on the line until the last speck of dust had been beaten from the rug.

Women and girls would wash the windows inside and out, with some arguments. "That streak is on your side." "No, I scrubbed hard at it. It's on your side."

All the pictures would be taken from the wall: George Washington, President Harding, two horses drinking from a trough and named *The Temperance Society*, Edna's parents' wedding picture, and a framed calendar picture of cows in a pasture. One of the aunts would carefully wash the glass and polish the frames, and after stacking the pictures on the porch, would warn the children not to run into them.

Edna would wash the painted walls, and vow that when she could afford it, she'd put wallpaper on so she wouldn't have to wash them again. The bag of rags from the attic and the Fels-Naptha soap would get heavy use all day. Edna would scrub the floor on her hands and knees, using a scrub brush. When the floor dried she might decide it needed a coat of varnish. Some of the stands might get varnished, too, while the brush was out and the can was open.

Along with this frenzy of activity, three meals would be put on the table that day and cleaned up after. No baking or roasting would be done, but there'd be plenty of leftovers for cold sliced meat and potato hash, and salad to go with the leftover baked beans. Gram would bring a couple of jars of pickles up from the cellar shelves. There would be a big bowl of applesauce, homemade bread, pies, cakes, and doughnuts.

There were no sandwich meals on busy days in the 1920s. If Edna had given Tom a sandwich and told him that was the noon meal, he might not have divorced her, but he would have let her know what her duties were.

Edna's ability to predict the weather held; the sun shone and the wind blew all day, and everything dried. After supper everybody carried something back to the room. Then they all stared at the shining windows, the starched, ruffled white curtains, the clean flowered cretonne covers. And oh, the smell!

There were no spray cans back then to hide bad odors and make a room smell like flowers. The sitting room smelled as clean as soap and water and as sweet as cotton blowing on the clothesline in the wind and the sunshine.

Surprisingly the room would stay clean for a long time, with weekly dustings and sweepings. Men's work clothes and boots came off in the shed, and children went into the room only if their shoes were clean. Nobody smoked in the room. Men enjoyed their pipes outdoors in good weather, in the kitchen during the winter. Nobody ate or drank in the room. Those wanting a bedtime snack sat at the kitchen table. When the women had a morning rest with a doughnut and a cup of coffee, or an afternoon cup of tea and a cookie, they sat on the porch or in the kitchen. Since there were two Aladdin lamps on stands in the sitting room, Tom sat in the good light and read the Bangor paper or *The Country Gentleman*. Women used the light for knitting, crocheting, darning, and patching. By the mid-1920s a radio appeared on a stand, and the family laughed at *Amos 'n' Andy*.

Although the other rooms endured spring cleaning also, they didn't cause the stir that the sitting room did. Life on the farm went at its normal pace until on another April day, Edna again uttered those fateful words.

# 13

# The Joys of Imperfection

I'VE NEVER BEEN CALLED a perfect anything—well, idiot, maybe. In my first-grade class picture my legs were apart, my dress wadded up between them. My knees were scratched and scabbed. I had somehow lost my hair ribbon—it may have been in the tree I climbed at recess—and my hair was in my eyes.

After all these years, the trend continues. Recently a woman sitting beside me at our book group confided that she'd had a brown spot removed from her face. "I think it's important to look as close to perfect as possible—don't you agree?"

I choked back a laugh. She must not have noticed that I had so many brown spots I could be dubbed Polka Dotty! Years ago a woman in a commercial said she could no longer play bridge with her friends because she was so ashamed of the brown spots on her hands. The ad promised that a magic cream would remove the spots. Sometimes when I look at the brown spots on my hands and arms, I see pictures—a fish, or the Big Dipper. I find that interesting.

"No, no," the book group facilitator said, when I shared my thoughts with her. "Your face—what feature do you like best?"

Hmmm . . . Not my eyes, because one turns in a little. The doctor who fitted my first pair of glasses had me do exercises with a pencil held at a distance and slowly moved toward my face. I did them, but they didn't help.

And not my mouth, which is crooked. Only two teeth touch together. My lower lip is too fat, and my chin is weak and receding. For years I tried to smile while pulling in my lower lip, sticking my chin out and twisting my jaw to even things up.

In the 1930s a winsome smile was important in the game of winkum. A smile and a wink were supposed to cause a boy sitting in the circle to pull away from the girl standing behind him, and bound over to the empty chair in front of me. All my smiles and winks didn't produce many boys in my empty chair.

So, what's left? I had never thought much about my nose, but I didn't hate it, so that's what I chose.

Then there were my less-than-perfect clothes. I grew up happy in faded, made-over, comfortable dresses, but once on my own, mistakes abounded. My college boyfriend said the first thing he noticed about me walking across campus was my bulky orange tweed suit purchased at an Ellsworth five-and-ten. Aside from being an ugly suit, the bottom of the skirt was so tight that I had to toe in and walk like a duck. Don found that hilarious.

In a college class I sewed a blue chiffon evening gown and hemmed it to within a few inches from the floor. The first time I wore it, the skirt stretched until both my partner and I were dancing on it. I hemmed it again. It stretched again, and again we danced on it. I hated to give up on that dress, for until it stretched, I'd felt elegant wearing it.

Now in old age I will live happily in my soft, warm old sweatpants and sweatshirts, and be glad to see my crooked smile in the mirror each morning—proof that, faults and all, I've been given another day.

# 14

# Rural Aroostook Women

I MET THEM FIRST IN 1941 when I married Don Smith
and moved to a potato farm in Aroostook County. I grew up
in a downstate village of women who were good cooks and
housekeepers, even during the Depression, yet they often
seemed tired and discouraged. It was amazing to see Aroostook women who scrubbed and waxed every floor in their
houses weekly, did their cooking from scratch, and hand-
scrubbed their families' clothes. They laughed so much I had
to believe they were having fun, no matter how hard they
worked. I couldn't imagine women so strong, so healthy, so
energetic.

There was Augusta Mahaney, known as Gustie. She and her
husband Luman were kind to me in my early insecure years in
Easton. They lived on a farm, but found time to be good citizens, participating in community activities and attending all
school functions.

Gustie always looked stylish and beautiful, and I never
heard her complain or saw her when she wasn't smiling. If
they chaperoned senior prom, Luman and Gustie danced
every dance. It was obvious they had a good time together, no
matter what they did. One night I watched her and wondered
how she could be so sparkling. Maybe she had help at home,
I thought. Surely she had done nothing that day more diffi-
cult than painting her nails. Then she sat down near me and I

listened to her conversation, which went something like this: "I got up earlier than usual this morning and got my house-work done up because I knew Luman needed me in the potato house for most of the day."

How could she do all that and look so fresh and peppy? How could she shed that potato dirt so quickly and completely?

She was one of many Aroostook superwomen. I remember Lydie Mullen who had a family of big, husky, fun-loving boys. This was before the days of clothes dryers and drip-dry fabrics. What a stack of work, school, and dress shirts she must have washed and ironed every week, and what a lot of cooking and dishwashing, as well as cleaning. Yet she always looked as if she were having a great time, whether at home, or helping to serve a church supper or town meeting dinner.

I recall a story she told me: One Sunday morning she left wood in the stove and a chicken in the oven, so it would be hot for dinner when she returned from church. However, the boys came home, smelled the chicken, decided they couldn't wait for dinner, and ate the whole thing. Then they put the bones back together and returned them to the oven. How Lydie laughed when she told of finding the skeleton in her roasting pan. I don't know what the Mullen family had for dinner that day, but I'm sure it was plentiful and tasty.

Early on I saw an example of the kindness of these women I admired so much. A new young Cooperative Extension agent had come to the County, eager to be helpful to the farm women who attended the meetings for socializing, as well as the chance to learn something new. At her first meeting the new agent demonstrated how to make a simple casserole—it might have been a potato or corn scallop. She talked about its nutritional value, and what to serve with it. She demonstrated in great detail the process of making it, using many unnecessary cooking dishes and many pointless, tedious steps.

She didn't know that every woman there often made that casserole in half the time, with a baby on one hip and an eye on the kids playing in the dooryard. Perhaps her husband had asked her to drive to town to pick up a part for the tractor, or maybe she'd made trips to the garden for fresh vegetables for a salad, yet, no matter what, the meal was on the table at the right time and everything tasted great. But those women let none of their experience show when they thanked the agent for coming and praised her casserole. She was doing the best she could, bless her heart. She'd learn in time.

I don't recall ever hearing back then that these Aroostook women went with their families on expensive vacations. If the Easton High School basketball team went to a tournament, they might go to Bangor, stay in a hotel, eat in restaurants, and do a little shopping during the weekend.

At home they didn't eat out frequently. Several families might get together on a Saturday night, each woman bringing her specialty, which resulted in a great meal. Then they might play cards, or sometimes charades, which caused great hilarity. An onlooker would have suspected they were all intoxicated. Actually, there was little or no drinking in the homes of farm families I knew, although sometimes the men went on hunting trips and came home with funny and probably exaggerated tales of their drinking escapades. Like the women, Aroostook men also laughed a lot and seemed to love what they were doing.

I am grateful that I experienced Aroostook in the 1940s, and met so many women who became my heroes and role models. Although I tried to emulate them, I often goofed up.

Once, for instance, I made a cake, which I wanted to be impressive. It was a chocolate cake with a fluffy white boiled frosting. I placed it on a white platter, put a ribbon around it, and then added a wide row of flowers. It was gorgeous—it looked like a wide-brimmed hat with floral decorations.

Unfortunately, I didn't soak the pink, blue, and white bachelor buttons, so when I served the cake, little ants had traveled from the flowers up into the white frosting. I got teased about that for a long time.

In later years, I've met younger Aroostook women—some of them daughters and granddaughters of my 1940s heroes—who have the strength, energy, and optimism of their forebears. Maybe it's something innate to the area. Maybe the magic in the soil that produces such great potatoes also produces great women.

# 15

# The Mattress Matter

I WONDER HOW THEY SLEPT—my great-many-greats gramp and gram who lived in caves. After Gramp clubbed Gram and dragged her by the hair to bed, what did they sleep on? Animal skins, maybe. I wonder if they fought over the coverings on a cold night. We can trace the progress or the deterioration of the human race by considering the substances on which they slept.

In my genealogy, the perfect bed existed at the turn of the century, and was created by my great-grandmother, Addie Lassell. She raised the geese, plucked them of their downy feathers, sold them for meat, and stuffed the feathers into ticking covers she had sewn. These feather ticks she piled onto straw mattresses which rested on wooden slats. Sometimes there would be three ticks on one bed, making it necessary to climb up little stairs in order to fall down into them. And oh, the sensation as I sank down into feathers which wrapped around me. In a minute I was so warm and comfy that I didn't want to move until daybreak. It was painful to climb out and down the steps into a cold morning.

I can't even guess at the hours of work that went into producing those beds, and maintaining them. Once every summer Gram picked a calm day, opened the ticking, put the feathers into barrels, washed the ticks by hand, dried them on the line, refilled them, sewed the ends, and piled them back on the beds. Since they were covered with blankets and sheets, I don't know why the ticking had to be washed every year. Gram was amazing. Not only did she work harder than anyone I ever knew, she was also the best cook and housekeeper, and had more fun than any of my other ancestors seemed to. She loved to play cards, write funny poems, joke with friends, dress up, and go visiting.

I have slept on many surfaces since the feather ticks, but nothing has ever been so comfortable. For a while I slept on a heated water bed, but that era ended in a leak that flooded the bedroom. I was lucky I didn't get electrocuted in my sleep. Once I slept in a motel where after inserting a quarter, the bed jiggled up and down for a few minutes. While chaperoning school trips I have climbed into a sleeping bag on a gym floor. If I'm tired enough I can sleep anywhere—even on the torturous seats of a school bus.

I marvel, however, at the lengths some mattress companies will go to sell their product. One ad features an actress who explains to the viewers that if we are not sleeping on something called a sleep-number bed, we have never known true bliss. I don't see how she can keep a straight face and say such silly things.

In another ad an attractive young couple is sleeping on a queen-size bed. The narrator explains that the two sides of the bed are wired differently, so she can make her side softer and warmer while her hardy hero can make his side firmer and colder. How my cave ancestors would laugh! The young couple looks at each other with such ardor that you know they are going to have a wonderful time in that changeable bed.

Then there is an old couple in a bed in which the front or the back or the middle cranks up to contort them into shapes that look thoroughly uncomfortable, yet they grin and pretend they love it.

Why do we work so hard to make something as simple as a night's sleep such a production?

# 16

# I Love Coffee

"I LOVE COFFEE, I LOVE TEA, I love the boys and the boys love me." As a little girl I jumped rope to that ditty. I didn't start drinking coffee, however, until I was a freshman in college and needed to stay awake late and cram for tests. In my busy years I had a cup going most of the time. Now I allow myself one cup (one large mug) per day. I like coffee at all temperatures—iced in summer, hot enough in winter to keep my hands warm. Because the taste is best when the brew is just lukewarm, I am tempted to gulp—but I still sip.

As long as I am sitting here sipping coffee, nobody will drop in and think, "Look at the lazy old thing—just sitting there, doing nothing." My cup in hand tells them that as soon as I finish my morning coffee I'll get up and fly around, doing important stuff.

As long as there's coffee in the cup, I can sit here and watch the chickadees flitting around my trees. I look forward to the return of the crows of March. I like to talk with crows.

I glance into my big yellow mug—now close to empty. Must sip more slowly. I love the color of coffee with milk. Basketball player Ray Allen is that color, a more beautiful people color than darker black or pale white. Maybe someday the races will have intermingled to a point where everybody is coffee-colored. We will all look healthier, and besides, that will end racial turmoil.

As long as the coffee lasts I can stare around the room at all the family pictures. I haven't exactly founded a dynasty, but the few descendants I have are all without flaw. Since I have a long list of faults, it's amazing that my sons are perfect and my grandchildren are close to perfect.

I have sipped through the TV morning show from which I learned about the star who wore a revealing dress to a gala. Then I hear the sneers of the woman who sets herself up as the fashion maven of the universe. Now the show is over and I still have a few more sips.

My neighbor is shoveling snow. She works much harder than I do. Shovel—a well-named tool for shoving stuff around.

I hate to be shoved around. Back when JFK was running for president he made an airport stop at the former air base in Presque Isle. My friend and fellow teacher, Avis Lamoreau, a Democrat in this then-Republican stronghold, persuaded me to go to the airport to see him. We rushed up right after school and tall Avis angled through the crowd, dragging me along behind. Finally we made it to a rope which held people back from the walkway that led from the plane to the podium. Avis was determined to shake the hand of the presidential hopeful as he walked by. But then the rope barricade was changed and we were roughly elbowed away. Not accustomed to such treatment, I was shocked. I learned later that the committee in charge kept making changes because they were terrified that some rabid Republican would shoot the president-to-be.

We listened to his speech, which was short, his gestures, awkward. Later I read that Mr. Kennedy was taking lessons in speechmaking.

Earlier that day the high school principal had requested that a group of boys be dismissed so they could go to the base to park cars for the visit. Some teachers advised Don and me that we shouldn't let Steve go to see that Democrat, yet he wanted to go, and we allowed it. It had been rumored that Jackie would step out of the plane and make an appearance, but that didn't happen. When the boys, hoping for a glimpse of Jackie, started up the steps of the plane, they were quickly dispatched. I'm not sure if shoving took place.

During the war, famous people often stopped at Presque Isle on their way overseas to entertain the troops. Several people mentioned seeing Bing Crosby. A woman I knew saw Clark Gable at a hotel in Presque Isle. She said he had shoved a woman aside so he could get to a phone first. After that, he was not my hero.

If I were famous I'd have bodyguards to keep me from being pushed around. Years ago, on my one trip to Macy's in New York City, I saw Greta Garbo walking along, wrapped in a camel-hair coat with the collar turned up. I think there were four bodyguards surrounding her. The salespeople were point-ing and whispering her name. I was in awe of her; I was will-ing to keep my distance even without the bodyguards.

Another tiny sip. My neighbor Marla brought me home-made peanut-butter balls. They go great with coffee. The tele-phone rings. When I find it is a canned message, I hang up. I hate to hang up on a real person, but sometimes I am forced to when I have said "no" four or five times and the caller still persists.

"Oh, I see your point, Mrs. Smith, but I'm sure that when you understand our cause, you will be glad to—"

Since I'm not smart enough to tell sincere people from cons, I usually reserve my giving for charities I'm sure of. Even so, if I donated to every worthy cause, my old cat and I would have to stop eating.

The sips are getting smaller and further apart. Soon I will face that dreaded empty cup, the harbinger of facing up to another day. And it's still early—oh my gosh, it's 1:20. Land sakes, where does the time go?

# 17

# My Horrible Day

I'VE JUST HAD A TERRIBLE DAY. I want to call a dear friend and tell her about it, but I can't do that. She'll say, "Oh, are you ill?" I'll have to say no. If only I could say I'm all broken out with hives or I think I have rickets, she'd sympathize with me. Then she'll ask if I have fallen, had an accident. Again, no. She'd be sad if I could say I fell down the cellar stairs and broke both legs. But I'd be lying. I could say that the furnace blew up and there's a layer of ashes on everything. Or that I ran my car into an old man who was crossing the street with his walker and he's going to sue me.

There are many valid reasons for a terrible day, but none of them happened to me.

Still, it was an awful day. To begin with, the sun was shining and I wanted to hurry through my chores and go for a walk. Then I planned to drive to the post office and the grocery store before going to my Wednesday Group.

I pull on a beautiful red turtleneck, jeans, and a cozy sweater. I brush my hair, which is very long. At home I let it hang or I put it in a ponytail, but when I go out, I try to look my age. I put it in an elastic, wind it up tight, and secure it with a hair clip. It doesn't look particularly good, but it's quick, it's grandmotherly, and it's usually neat

But this morning I can't find my favorite clip. On my bed stand? No. Beside my recliner? No. On a bathroom shelf?

No. I know I'll find it, so I hunt for a long time. I don't find it. However, I have other clips in a drawer. Surely one of them will work. I clip one into my hair and sit down to pay a couple of bills and write a note before going to the post office. Then my hair sags down. The clip won't hold. I brush again and choose another clip.

When I return to my desk I feel as if the turtleneck is choking me. I tug, trying to loosen it. I try to ignore it. Finally I take it off, and go to one of my turtleneck bins for another one. Someday I'll count my turtlenecks. I'll bet I have seventy-five, or maybe a hundred. I've been wearing them for seventy years and I don't remember throwing any away. I keep buying new ones at half-price sales and yard sales. Pulling the sweater off causes the clip to fly off and break. I brush again and choose another clip. My arm is getting tired from brushing.

As soon as I put the next turtleneck on—a blue one with a loose neck which feels too loose right away—the clip falls off and I have to brush again. I want to have a temper tantrum, but I'm almost ninety, for goodness' sake. "Suck it up, Glenna," I mutter.

I finish the bills and the note, and reach for my little address book. It isn't there on the desk. It may be on the table beside my recliner. It isn't there. Quickly I blame Mr. Gray, who walks across the table on his way to my lap. He always gets in my lap to warm his feet after he has been outdoors. If he is in a playful mood, he will pitch a couple of things from the table to the floor. Maybe he pushed the book into my knitting basket. I empty everything out. No little pink book. Maybe it fell into the basket of old newspapers. I empty the basket and put the papers in the bag for the recycle. Still no pink book. Maybe he knocked it under the couch. I run the broom handle under there and encounter no objects. I look on all the bookshelves.

I'm beginning to panic. I have no backup for all those addresses and cell-phone numbers. Some of my old friends would be lost to me if I lost their addresses. I want to sit down and cry, but I don't often cry about real things. I cry at old movies and high school marching bands and—

Just then the phone rings and I hear the voice of a dear friend.

She asks what I'm doing.

"Absolutely nothing," I snarl. She misses the snarl.

"Oh, good," she says. "I have this problem and—"

I want to yell, *I don't want a problem! If I wanted a problem, I'd take a math course, and I hate math! Just take your old problem and put it—*

Of course I don't say it. Her feelings would be hurt. No, I believe she would think that Glenna never screams at people, so she must be losing her mind. She would come to help. I smile. Then I think, *What if I am going crazy?* Maybe I'll find the little book in the freezer compartment or in my underwear drawer or at the bottom of the laundry basket. I look in all those places. Tomorrow I'll call son Mel and tell him that he and brothers Steve and Barney had better make plans to put me in a safe place, because I can no longer cope. But I can't call Mel; I don't have his cell-phone number. I'm the only one in the family who can't remember numbers.

Just then my hair slips down again. It has been years since I visited a hair-cutting place, but I'll find one tomorrow. I will have my head shaved and wear a stocking hat for the rest of the winter. Then I'll find a nice gray wig. Oh, what the heck. I'll find a red one.

I take a deep breath. I remember that I had saved the obituary page of the *Bangor Daily News* because I needed the address of an old friend's charity of choice. I put it right here by the lamp. It isn't here. Could I have put it in the bag with all of February's papers, and March's, so far?

I empty the bag on the living-room floor. My cat Coty thinks it's a game. She rolls on the papers and throws some of them in the air. I go through all of the papers until I find the obit. I feel sad, looking at the lovely picture of a woman I've known for years, although she was a bit older than I am. When we ancients go, it's in the scheme of things. I repack the papers. I can't believe how much of the day I've wasted.

No time now for a walk in the sunshine or a trip to the grocery store. I'll go to the post office on my way to Wednesday Group: a social gathering. I brush my falling-down hair again and try more clips. Maybe I should stay home. No, I'll wear a stocking hat if necessary.

I enjoyed my friends at the group, but my hair kept slipping, and I wondered if I'd ever see my pink book again. Later I shared a pleasant dinner with another friend, and almost dreaded going home. When I entered the house I looked sadly at my sleeping cats. *What will happen to them when I have to be committed?* Perhaps we can sell the house to someone who will understand that the cats own house and grounds.

I remember that the Celtics are playing. Good. That will take up my mind. Oh no! Still the first period, and they are more than twenty points behind. Coach Doc Rivers looks about the way I feel.

I can't stand any more sadness, so I turn the TV off. I sit in a rocking chair and spy the broken pieces of my favorite hair clip. Then on another table atop a stack of magazines I see two small books. The top one is a mystery paperback. I don't recognize the other book, with a dark brown spine. I lift the paperback—and there's my little pink address book! I didn't know it had a brown spine. I'd looked at those two books a dozen times during my earlier search. My old friends are not lost to me after all.

Surely I'll find another perfect hair clip somewhere, so nothing really terrible happened on this awful day.

Well, I'm not too sure about the going-crazy part. As we'd left the restaurant I'd looked under the table and asked Mary, "Where's my cane?"

I was leaning on it at the time.

# 18

# Predictions

IT HAPPENS BECAUSE Byron Smith takes the shortcut on his way home. A carpenter living in Washington County, he turns off onto Pocomoonshine, a road connecting Routes 1 and 9. He looks at the moon reflected in the middle of the pond, and thinks about the coming pool tournament. He says to himself, "I hope I play better than I did last week." Just then he hits a spot of black ice and his pickup spins around, leaves the road, rolls over, and finally lands driver's side down. Bruised and shaken, he finds he isn't bleeding, and as far as he can tell, no bones are broken.

Then he realizes he'd just been out of control. He had been a safe driver for fifty years or so, and had always thought he'd be in complete control of his vehicle. Now a small patch of invisible ice had shown him his vulnerability.

He unhooks his seat belt, reaches up, and manages to open the door on the passenger side. He climbs up and out, and finds he's a few hundred yards from the Green Thumb Greenhouse. He walks to the home of the owners, Francis and Claire Wallace, and asks if he may use their phone to report his accident to the police. The answering officer asks if he is hurt, and when he says no, he is told that two accidents have just been called in, both involving injuries. He asks Byron if he can stay where he is until they can get to him. The Wallaces agree that he may stay, and with them he watches the History Channel.

The program is at first about the predictions of Nostradamus, French astrologer born in 1503. Some people believe that many of his predictions have already come about; others maintain that his language is so vague, they can't be sure. It is known that Nostradamus created a calendar which was to end in 2012.

Next the program switched to the Mayans on the Yucatan peninsula, who by the beginning of the Christian era had also created a calendar to end in 2012. Then it was reported that the Hopi Indians, peace-loving farmers and shepherds in Arizona and surrounding areas, also had a calendar not predicted to go beyond 2012. Since many early civilizations developed calendars based upon their understanding of astrology and astronomy, it is not unusual that this agreement would exist. The predicted event which they believed would bring about change at that time: a lining up of magnetic fields in a way that happens every two or three thousand years.

It may be that this change in gravitational pull will for a time allow more meteorites to enter our atmosphere. The Hopi believed that changes in our technological world would allow them to reclaim the life they'd had before the migration of the white race took over their territories.

Byron, who lives one day at a time, wasn't duly upset, but he did find it coincidental that, on a day when his world (his Dodge pickup, anyway) had turned upside down, he found himself watching a program about possible upsets in the big world.

He thinks about it, and then writes a poem to which he adds a drawing of a buffalo from his sketchbook. The buffalo's world has also changed for the worse since the advancing of white civilization. True, Byron and all of us accept that we cannot halt technological changes; if we can invent it and build it, we'll create a use for it.

We're all a bit out of control with our world today, yet perhaps these predictions will make us think, as Byron did, of the frailty of life. Perhaps we will learn to treasure each day, have more thought for our fellow humans, and for the creatures who, like us, feel fear and pain and loss. How great it would be if all of us had the freedom to run in the sunshine, and to sleep in peace in the moonshine.

# Part Three:

# Getting Older

# 19

# Retire

THE WORD RETIRE SUGGESTS A VARIETY of meanings: It could refer to something a mechanic does to a wheel; it could involve becoming weary again; it often means going to bed. If a woman has a retiring personality, she is shy. Commonly it means leaving one's lifelong career, attending a sad chicken dinner, and receiving a plaque.

Yet even that retirement has a variety of meanings. I have heard wives say they hated when their husbands retired because they were always around, underfoot. Another couple had a different experience.

Anna said to Joe, "You're retired, but I have to do the same old, same old." When he asked what chores she'd like to be rid of, she told him she was sick of planning meals, shopping for groceries, and cooking. "Then I'll take those jobs over," he said. It turned out that he loved preparing gourmet meals, so they were both happy.

I was surprised at my own reaction to retirement. Often during my busy years I'd daydream about what I would do after I no longer had a regular work schedule: I'd start reading a book in the morning, and with coffee and lunch breaks, I'd read all day. I'd go downtown and do errands in the daytime. I could watch US Open tennis all day and all evening. I could take a long afternoon nap and sit up until all hours, reading, writing, painting, or crocheting. Every day when the sun shone

I'd wash my sheets and dry them on the line. Then I'd always sleep in soft sheets that smelled of sunshine and wind. What a luxury!

Although I enjoyed my fantasies, I never really wanted to retire. I hurried to get to Presque Isle High School early every morning. I loved my students and my classes, enjoyed traveling with cheerleaders, going to drama competitions, chaperoning Hi-Y YMCA youth group trips, biology field trips, French Club trips to Quebec, and once to France. When I reached seventy I still had enthusiasm for all my activities, but lacked the energy to do them well. My body told me it was time to make way for a younger teacher.

On the last day in my classroom—the day after school closed in the spring—I cleaned out my desk, file cabinets, closets, and bookcases. I packed up my houseplants, books, pictures, posters, extra sweaters and shoes, pens and pencils— my accumulation of twenty years there. I filled several garbage containers. I filled my car. I shed tears. I went home exhausted and fell into bed.

The next morning, a weekday, I awoke at the usual time, showered, ate my usual nutritious but quick breakfast, and—

Now what? The day was empty. No bells rang to tell me what class to expect next. I could have sorted out all the stuff I'd brought home from school—but I couldn't face that chore yet. I decided to have another cup of coffee. I poured it, but it didn't taste as good as the first one. I told myself that I should clean the house, but I didn't sound very convincing. *I know! I'll make a pan of brownies*, I thought. I had some vanilla ice cream in the freezer—No! Then I'd sit there and eat the whole pan.

I stared out the window and thought about my seventy years, fifty-five of which had been spent in schoolrooms. The first five were spent at home until I was school-age; later, I spent a happy ten years on the farm with my preschool little boys. On all the other Septembers I was either a student or a teacher. All those summers were busy and happy, too: cooking meals, taking care of my boys, watching them play Little League baseball, working on the farm when needed, taking summer classes—

But this summer was empty. Sons grown up, marriage ended in divorce, farmland sold, no need for summer courses, no schoolhouse in the fall.

Then who would I be? Always I'd had a title: Seth and Kathleen's little girl, Don's wife, Steve's and Barney's and Mel's mom, schoolteacher in Easton, Fort Fairfield, Presque Isle. Maybe I'd invent a degree: Glenna Smith, DWW (Done Working Woman). Perhaps I'd just be treading water until I died.

I stared out the window. I cried. The day dragged on.

I told myself to snap out of it. I'd call a friend. I picked up the phone, but couldn't think of anyone to call. Most of my friends were younger colleagues with husbands and children at home. I'd been so involved at school that I'd lost touch with friends my own age, many of whom still had husbands and busy lives of their own. I sat and stared.

I'd go to the grocery store. But the thought of food disgusted me.

The sun was shining. I'd go for a walk. I thought of all those pleasant mornings when I'd walked to school.

I cried again.

Then the telephone rang and Herb Andrews at Northeast Publishing told me that his proofreader had retired. He asked if I'd like to have the job. "Yes!" I told him. He said it didn't pay much, and I said that didn't matter. He asked when I could start and I said, "Tomorrow morning, early." I went to bed happy, feeling I'd been saved from falling into an abyss.

I enjoyed proofreading, I liked my coworkers, and I got interested in the production of a newspaper. Previously I had taken a summer course in which we'd traveled to all the sites where trees were cut, transported to a mill, and finally turned into huge rolls of newsprint. Now I saw the continuation of the process: ad gathering, layout, putting the paper together. Once I sat up all night watching the magic of the giant press changing those rolls of newsprint into printed words, and even color pictures. Before daybreak I watched the papers bagged and loaded onto trucks. Many people work hard to ensure that we Mainers have our morning paper. I gained great respect for reporters, editors, and newspaper workers at every level. I'm glad that in my lifetime newspapers won't be entirely replaced by electronic devices.

I left proofreading to substitute for a teacher at University of Maine at Presque Isle. Later I found a variety of activities to keep me busy. I led Elderhostel classes in life writing, I helped a friend direct plays at PIHS, I helped another friend with costumes for a summer theater in Skowhegan, I became involved with SAGE (college classes held at UMPI during April and October for those of us who are over fifty-five).

As the decades passed, I became aware of the wonderful gift of time. Time with family, my mainstay; time to have a role in the growing up of grandchildren; time to watch Red Sox and Celtics games; time for visits with dear friends; time to relish every day in my little house with my cats.

Now at age ninety I am slowing down. I haven't yet spent an entire day reading a book, and I don't wash my sheets every day. However, I have found more joyful moments in my decades of retirement than I could have ever imagined. So far I haven't fallen into the abyss, although I know it's still out there, and sometimes I must work to avoid it.

I still shudder when I recall that first day of retirement .

# 20

# Beware the Parabens

I WISH I HAD HEARD THE ENTIRE AD, but when I turn
on the TV, the beautiful blonde in the lab coat is in mid-sen-
tence. She is flashing a wide smile. (And no wonder. She must
have spent plenty on that mouthful of big, shiny white teeth.)
Yet she sounds worried. Looking down at a small carton in her
hand, she says, "And we guarantee that this product is free of
parabens . . . we know you want to protect yourself and your
household . . . becoming more and more of a threat . . . be
sure to read the fine print."

That confuses me. Companies who market products for
us old people put directions in print so small that even with
triple-vision glasses, good light, and a magnifying glass, I still
can't always make them out. Even when I *can* read them, there
are all those seven-syllable words I can neither pronounce nor
find in the dictionary.

I sip my coffee and watch the news, but I can't put parabens
out of my mind. I reach for the nearest dictionary, a well-used,
tattered one. Honestly, I think there's far more that I don't
know compared to the average person, and the older I get, the
less I understand. I find lots of *para-* words, but no *parabens.*
I try *-ben,* since *para-* is a prefix, Nothing. Maybe it's a brand
name, or a newly invented or discovered threat.

I suspect that somewhere there are hundreds of laboratories
filled with microscopes, telescopes, and PhDs trying to find

something new that will scare me to death. And there are other secret sites where super-brains are coming up with the multisyllabic words to counteract the bad ones. The war of syllables, that's what we need. Makes more sense than sending our young men and women off to a land they've never heard of, to kill or be killed.

I need breakfast. I pour a bowl of whole-grain cereal that contains dried strawberries. I can't help wondering if there are any parabens in it. I dust off the magnifying glass and squint at the fine print. Lots of ribo-ascorbo-palmetto stuff, but no parabens. It all sounds lethal, though. Oh, well, it tastes good, and I've lived for more than ninety years, so what have I got to lose? I'll eat it.

I look at the other side of the cereal box and see that the makers must think we buyers are stupid. There in big print I read NO ARTIFICIAL FLAVORS OR COLORS. All those ingredi-ents with the long names grow in nature? I doubt it. And I don't remember seeing any of them in the periodic table of chemical elements, so they must be plants. Maybe pyridoxine bushes don't grow around here.

Once someone said to me, "Don't eat any food that con-tains something you can't pronounce." Back in the 1920s most of our food was grown in the village or caught in the bay, and our mothers knew and could pronounce everything they added to the basics. If I wanted a snack I might go to the garden and pull up a carrot. I would wash off most of the dirt under the pump. Other stuff that I picked—wild blueber-ries, strawberries—I ate without washing. Growing up, I must have eaten a good amount of dirt and weeds, but a paraben wouldn't have stood a chance.

After I wash my dishes I wonder if I should spray the countertops with Lysol—but maybe parabens are tougher than Lysol. I telephone a friend.

"I heard about parabens on TV," I tell her.

"What's a paraben?" she asks.

"I hoped you knew," I say.

Somebody must know what they are. I can't ask my doctor. I hear all those ads—everything from laxatives to sex-drive enhancers—which state, "Ask your doctor if this product is right for you." Doctors must be tired of these questions.

It seems to me that the ad makers don't know much about sex. They seem to think that two naked people sitting in two bathtubs on a beach is a great come-on. I mean, really.

Do I eat or drink something containing parabens? Do I breathe it in, or do I rub it on? It may be in my hand lotion. I'll check. Active ingredients contain octocrylene, among others, and there are fourteen lines of inactive ingredients in tiny print. In big print: SPF 15, vitamins A, C, and D, plus antiaging antioxidants. Do two *antis* cancel each other out and become one pro, like double negatives? If not, my hands may stay young while the rest of me ages. Warnings in tiny, crowded lines include CALL DOCTOR IF RASH DEVELOPS; KEEP OUT OF REACH OF CHILDREN.

Must be potent stuff. I can see why organic farmers I know make their own lotions. Guess I'd better buy from them.

At this point in my life, it's too late to wonder about all the products claiming to enhance my beauty. They probably don't work anyway, and I think some of them are downright dangerous. For instance, the cream that is guaranteed to take ten years off my face. If a ten-year-old girl rubbed it on, her face would disappear. That would be spooky.

My father told me that science will find all the answers, and that I should have nothing to do with the supernatural. So why do I have more wins at double solitaire when I call on Lady Luck and the souls of my card-playing ancestors for help? And why, when I wanted a certain pair of socks yesterday, and hunted and hunted and then gave up, did they appear this morning right there in the sock drawer? And why, when I asked my granddaughter Hillary to find out what was wrong with my computer, could she find nothing wrong? Who can prove that there are no mischievous gremlins living here with me?

I can believe in them more easily than I can believe politicians who say that once they cut funds for social services and schools, and once they repeal environmental protection laws, our world will be a better place. It is easier to believe in the Great Pumpkin and the Easter Bunny.

Knowing so little about the workings of the real world, I must have blind faith in some people, like the ones who maintain my car and my furnace, and my doctor and pharmacist.

My faith must be well placed, for this morning, I've taken my pills and I feel great. The furnace hums, the car starts, and I've been given another day in which to find out what a *paraben* is.

# 21

# Requiem for a Giant

YESTERDAY I WITNESSED THE DEATH and destruction of a tree—a sixty-five-foot-tall maple across the street on Mary's lawn. I have admired this magnificent tree for all of the thirty-eight years I've lived here.

In the 1940s Coby Downing, owner of Downing Mills, built all the houses on my street. At that time two maple trees were planted on each lawn. Some of them have been cut down because the homeowners didn't like the trees; others may have been diseased. In all seasons and weather I admire those that remain. The two on my lawn are not in great condition. Once when some neighborhood lawns were dug up because of sewer trouble, many tree roots were cut.

The trees on Mary's lawn were the biggest and most beautiful because a former owner had fed them fertilizer. Mary loves her trees, but was recently informed by an expert that one was diseased and could fall on and damage her house. Thus yesterday was the dreaded day. I settled myself on my porch, knowing I must see everything no matter how painful.

Mid-morning on a perfect fall day, the heavy equipment came rolling in: a tractor with a scoop, a truck with a long, black, high-sided body, and a pickup. Men with hard hats swarmed around, carrying rakes. One man climbed to the top of the doomed tree and with his ax cut branches that fell to earth in great clumps, looking like smaller trees growing on the lawn. The black metal claws grabbed up the clumps and loaded them into the black hearse. How does it feel to be a tree of such permanence, suddenly having its limbs lopped off? I wish I had gone over to pick up a small branch with a few leaves; I could have dried it and put it on a wall. But I couldn't make myself move.

I noticed I wasn't the only observer. Others were standing outside their houses, staring. Younger homeowners, away at work and immersed in their own lives, may not have cared that the tree was being cut down.

One neighbor asked Mary, "Why don't you have the other one cut down while they're at it? It's too big. It dwarfs our houses." However, since the other was pronounced sound, it would remain for now. Soon the noisy, dusty stump shredder did its work, and that residue was piled on the truck. Then another truck arrived, carrying loam, which filled the hole. In a few weeks the grass seed will grow, and a newcomer will never know there was a tree there.

But I will know.

With the tree there, I could go up to my loft, look out the skylight, and feel that I lived in a tree house. I could see the many-shades-of-green leaves gently playing with the breeze or lashing frantically in a gale of wind. I could bask in red, orange, and gold autumn glory. I could watch the tracery of bare black branches on a winter sky. There is a big hole in my world, now that one of Mary's trees is no longer there.

Actually, I haven't looked out the window yet to see the space. I must do that.

But not today.

# 22

# Green Alligator Shoes

THE WIND IS HOWLING and rain is beating against the window. My car is safely tucked up in the garage, and I am cozy here in the house under layers of turtlenecks and sweaters. A good day to be home. A good day for a shopping spree. I pull on one more sweater and head upstairs where I pull boxes, bags, and trunks out of the crawl space.

Some bags haven't been opened for years. I tear into the first one, sure I'll find something I've forgotten and that I will love to wear again.

First thing I see is a favorite denim jacket, dark gray with big green roses all over it. I think I found it years ago at a flea market. It fit so well and was so wonderfully tailored that at first, I wore it often. Then one day a friend remarked that he couldn't imagine why anyone would buy a jacket with green roses on it. After that I didn't wear it when he was around. Finally, it ended up in a box somewhere. Several years later I wanted to wear it again, but I couldn't find it anywhere. I decided I must have left it somewhere while on a trip. I hoped that someone had found it who would love it as much as I had.

Years later Mel told me that when he'd moved some of his daughter's things from my garage attic, he must have taken one of my boxes by mistake. When Jasmine had opened her boxes, she discovered my things. I opened the box, not expecting much, but there on the top, looking as fresh and new as ever—my green-roses jacket. I hugged it. It was as if an old friend had died and been reborn. I hung it in the closet, determined to wear it often. Later it went back into a box.

But this time I really will wear it. I can never find anything green for St. Patrick's Day. Next March I'll wear the green jacket with my green alligator shoes. They're around here somewhere, in a carton of old shoes.

Years ago I felt I'd reached an age where I could walk safely only in sturdy sneakers. I'd donated all of my high-heeled shoes to the costume and prop room for the school's drama club, but couldn't part with the green alligator pair. I'd fallen in love with them at a secondhand shoe store. They had pointy toes and sassy, curved heels that weren't so very high, and they were, and still are, comfortable. When I wear them I feel wild, free, and very French. (After all, I had a lovely French great-several-greats-grandmother. I credit her genes with my love of life.)

I love looking at the green shoes. I've considered weighting the toes with bags of pennies and using them for bookends.

A few years ago I wore them to Mel's house on the Sunday before Halloween. I was a witch in a long black dress with a full skirt. I wore a black velvet hat and the shoes over black tights. I loved being a witch.

I burrow through a trunk and find the maroon evening gown I wore once in a Presque Isle Players production. I wonder why I saved that dress. And here's a pullover shawl I bought in Quebec City while chaperoning a French Club trip back in the '70s. The shawl was great for curling up with a good book on a cold night. This afternoon I'll wear it and curl up with that book I've been meaning to start.

Oh, here's the pumpkin with a light inside. I couldn't find it last Halloween. Now, where should I put it so I'll find it next year? And here's my NFL sweatshirt, so huge and fleece-lined. I wonder why I packed that away.

The telephone rings, and I hear the voice of my friend Louise. She says that since the sun has come out, she'll come to town to do some errands and visit her sister-in-law at Leisure Village. She asks if I want to go out to lunch. Surprised, I look out the window. The sun is almost shining. The clock says 11:30. I've spent all morning poking through boxes and daydreaming. I say, "Yes! I'd love to go to lunch."

Shall I wear the jacket with the roses? Not today. Tenderly I lay it in the trunk, along with the shawl, the shoes, and the sweatshirt. I tell them I know where to find them when I want them.

I wonder if a body can wear shoes when it's cremated. I wouldn't mind wearing the alligator shoes to wherever I'm going.

# 23

# Lost in the Real World

I NEED A CELL PHONE—one that flashes blue lights and plays a pretty tune. It should be easy to find a discarded one. I know people who often buy a new phone because of the latest trick it can perform. The thing is, I don't need one that works; I don't know anyone who wants to talk to me by the hour, and I don't need all the stuff the average consumer needs. When a phone can find where I left my glasses and feed the cats early in the morning when I want to sleep, then I might buy one. For now, I just need a play phone so I can feel I'm part of the human race.

One day last week, I saw, walking toward me and smiling, a former neighbor I haven't seen in years. I was eager to greet her and ask about the family. Then I saw she wasn't smiling at me; although I was there in that time and space, she was engaged in an excited conversation with someone who wasn't there. She walked by without seeing me. I walked on, feeling lonely and invisible.

My pretend phone would have helped me save face that day, and it would have many other uses, as well.

When I was a kid I had imaginary playmates. Why not an imaginary phone pal, dead or alive, real or fictional? I might call Tom Mix, cowboy hero of my youth.

"How are you, Tom?"

"Not very well. Once, thousands of kids loved me and my horse, Tony. Mention my name to a little boy today and he will mutter, 'Tom who?' He won't even look up from the game he's playing on that little gadget he carries around."

Tom needs a phone pal, and so does Clara Bow, the "It" girl of the 1920s who wore short flapper skirts, bobbed her hair, danced on tabletops, and poured champagne into her little satin slipper. Then her date would drink from the slipper. Shocking! Her deeds wouldn't make the papers today, what with the antics of all those rich young blondes who have captured the media. Yes, I'll talk to Clara about her bad-girl image in the good old days.

Then, there's my habit of talking to all things inanimate. I always say good morning to sun, sky, trees, and one crow I call Charlie. Charlie is the only one who answers. I could chat with any of them while holding a cell phone and the neighbors wouldn't think I was crazy.

Sometimes when away from home I'm forced to have a meal in a restaurant. I don't like to eat alone in public places; I never know where to look, or what to do with my hands between bites. With my cell phone I could talk to Tom and Clara and the moon and the stars.

I wonder if there are others like me who feel rejected in the cell-phone world. What if some of them are already walking around with fake phones glued to their ears?

That gray-haired man barking orders to an underling back at the office—what if there's neither office nor underling? What if he's just having trouble adjusting to retirement? Maybe he likes to pretend he's still in charge. And that young woman who is giggling and cooing and looking so lovesick; is she just wishing she had a boyfriend? And the older woman

complaining to the travel agent for messing up her trip schedule; maybe she could never afford a real vacation. And the
high school boy who's so bright that none of his classmates
will talk to him. He could invent a whiz of a phone pal.

What a drastic thought—that maybe some of the cell
phones on the street are fakes. And lucky for us have-nots; as
long as we chatter and smile and pause now and then on our
fake phones, nobody will be able to tell the difference.

# 24

# Has Anyone Seen John? Or Mary?

WHEN I WAS YOUNG we all knew who we were named
after—a relative or beloved friend, usually. All of us in my
grade school had names that had been around for a long time:
Robert, Elliott, and Stanley; Patricia, Emily, and Marion.
Robert might be called Bob; Patricia might be Patty—still predictable. Our dogs had conventional names, too: Spot, Shep,
King, and Rover were common.

Then came the revolution. New parents looked for new
names: Yellow, Skye, Apple, and River appeared. And by then
dogs were Millie, Tyler, or Rudy.

This lust for originality also spawned strange spellings:
Ellyn, Nanci, Jayne. I held a proofreading job during these
times. Convinced that most of the names of newborns were
typos, I'd call the homes and check.

"Her name really is Etheyle? Just checking!" It seems Dad
had wanted to name the child Ethel for his grandmother, but
Mom had considered that too old hat.

Then there was little Do-Do, pronounced *dough-dough*. I
wonder if when Do-Do gets her PhD in physics, she may
change her name to Doris? Doreen? Diane?

It is often confusing to have a name which can be used for
either sex, as with Jean or Jan. Once Don and I, chaperoning
students for a convention, had a shy boy named Jean in our
group. When he found out he had been assigned a roommate

named Betty, he rushed up to Don and asked him to make a change. Don, having a little joke, told the boy it was too late to make changes. Don realized how truly distressed the boy was when he demanded to leave the trip and return home. Changes were quickly made.

Sometimes on a list of new babies there isn't even a single one with a familiar name. None are named for somebody, none have ties to the past—they are all floating around in the new alphabet soup. Many a first-grade teacher has said to a new student, "Are you sure this is the right spelling?"

In our family, Don and I were guilty of nicknames. Steven became Steve, Byron became Barney, and Melbourne became Mel. When Barney entered one class and explained to the old and fearsome teacher that his family and everybody else called him Barney, she said, "You'll never be Barney in this room!" However, as soon as she decided she liked him, he became Barney again.

I sometimes thought that my granddaughters Jasmine, Ashley, and Hillary sounded more like Southern belles than rural Maine girls. However, I've grown to like their names. Ashley named her children Tim and Abby—admirable. And who knows? Maybe they will name their children John and Mary.

# 25

# The Grocery-Store Scooter Caper

WHEN A FRIEND TAKES ME SHOPPING I usually push the cart because I need to lean on it for balance. But today, because we did a few errands before going to the grocery store, my legs protest that they can go no farther. I suggest to Mary-Ann that I sit in the car while she does the shopping.

"Why don't you ride on one of those motorized scooters?" she asks.

"Oh, yes!" I say. "I've always wanted to do that."

We walk up to the line of vehicles and a smiling clerk brings a key. She points to what looks like the oldest of the lot, saying that this would be a good one for a first trip. The seat is comfortable, and I listen impatiently while she tells me that pushing this button sends me forward, that one backs me up. She asks if I have any questions. I want to tell her about my zooming down I-95 in my little Saab Sonnet. That was a long time ago, but surely I'll have no trouble with a motorized scooter.

I push the forward button and the thing jerks ahead rapidly. Before I can remove my hand I've hit the corner of the banana island. The bananas jump a bit, but don't fall to the floor. I'd better be careful around that next island with those stacks of oranges. That nice clerk will ground me if I spill them all.

Hastily I back up and hit a display of those little cans of cat food. Whew! Only a couple of cans fall to the floor. I hope one doesn't roll down the aisle where someone might trip on it, fall, and break a leg. I'll be sued. What if I have to go to jail? My grandchildren will be so ashamed. I can see now why the clerk gave me this old scooter. She wasn't thinking of my safety so much as the scooter's. It would be too bad to scratch one of those shiny, newer ones.

Oh, now I'm going in a straight line down the medicine aisle. I notice that products we old ones buy, like Metamucil and Efferdent, are within easy reach for the rider. Easy rider . . . that's me. Wish I had a helmet and goggles. Guess I can't go fast enough for a white scarf to blow in the wind. I should have a racing stripe and a Klaxon horn—or one of those musical horns that plays "How Dry I Am." Cars had great horns back in the 1920s.

Oops! I take a left turn into another aisle, and a young woman has to step lively to avoid being hit. Maybe there should be traffic lights at the ends of aisles. I drive by a young mother who has stopped to look at cereals. The cart she is pushing is a special one designed for kids, where the child sits underneath in a built-in "car." The little boy sitting in the car's seat is leaning forward and twisting his steering wheel, glaring at me for passing him. He presses an imaginary horn and says "Beep, beep." I beep right back at him.

Statistically, more and more of us are living to an advanced age. Maybe in a few years there'll be twenty or thirty old ones all driving scooters at once in the grocery store. Those walking won't stand a chance. Or maybe by then there will be geriatric grocery stores with no top shelves, smaller quantities of products, and with only easy-to-chew foods.

I've seen a couple of people in here driving scooters. If they were here today, we could play bumper cars. They might not

126

want to, though; they always look so dignified and in control
of their vehicles.

Mary-Ann is rushing to complete the list and get us out of
here. I wonder why she looks worried. I'm beginning to have
a great time, although I wish that I'd had a little driver's ed
course in backing up and turning. Perhaps we should have to
log a few hours in the parking lot before driving solo.

There, I'm back where we started.

"I hate to get out," I say. "I'm just getting the hang of it."

The bag boy grins. "Drive it out into the parking lot if you
want to," he says.

"Oh, thank you," I say, "but it won't go through the door."

"Sure it will," he says, "with room to spare."

I inch along, sure I'll get stuck, but he's right; there's plenty
of room. I wish now that we'd parked the car far from the
entrance so I could have a longer ride. I wish I could drive this
home and go up and down my street, visiting my neighbors. I
wish those other two riders were here—I'd challenge them to
a race.

# 26

# Glenna in Wonderland

I HATE TV ADVERTISING. I know that some of it is necessary, but I whine and complain anyway. I remember when I could watch a show that would be interrupted every fifteen minutes by a couple of commercials. I could live with that. Then the ads became longer, there were more of them, and they trivialized us human beings. I am sick of people finding love because they changed to the expensive shampoo, or because they lost twenty pounds while eating everything they wanted and just taking a magic pill, or when I see a husband who gets a big kiss only because he shells out for a diamond. One day I counted ads on several different channels, often a string of seven or eight, sometimes even ten.

Yet I adapted. At the first word of a commercial I would go to the kitchen and wash a few dishes, put a potato in to bake, or fix a snack. Or I might go to my bedroom and gather up some laundry. I could time it to get back to the program when it resumed.

But the admen couldn't accept defeat. There was a new tactic that I first saw while watching the Red Sox. Suddenly down near home plate a little divan appeared and the grinning man sitting on it hawked his wares. I called him names and told him where to go, but I couldn't get rid of him. He wasn't on long enough to allow for my usual during-ad housekeeping chores, and I didn't want to miss the game. Score one for the admen.

It gets worse. A few nights ago when the weatherman predicted a two-day blizzard, I settled into my recliner, snuggled under my afghan, and picked up the remote in search of a good movie. First I tried the classics channel, where I can watch a whole wonderful show with no ads, but I didn't want to watch the war epic about to start. On another channel I found a favorite Sandra Bullock movie that I've watched several times. I was in the mood to get lost in it again, share the problems of Sandra's character, and be with her at last when she finds love.

But what are those big white letters in the lower right-hand corner of the screen? They name Joan Rivers and her daughter and a program in which they will appear. The letters are so bright that I can't ignore them. I try closing one eye, turning my head, and squinting. That's better—but now what? Two tiny figures are leaping and grinning and pointing to the letters. They are Joan and Melissa, so bright and shining that they interfere with my mood. With regret I search for another program.

Maybe I'll find an *NCIS* or a *Law & Order* rerun. Yet there's an ad on each channel!

On one a man points to me and yells, "Act now! This offer will last only ten more minutes! For just three little payments of $99.99, this life-changing machine can be yours! It will come wrapped in plain brown paper so your neighbors will never know that you are walking mile after mile right there in your own game room! But soon they will notice the change in you."

A man with unbelievable muscles struts across the screen and says, "A month ago I was a ninety-seven-pound weakling!"

They flash to a picture of a weakling cowering before a bully.
"Now I am the terror of the neighborhood!" he proclaims.
They flash to him bullying a ninety-seven-pound weakling.
"Hurry!" he yells. "This offer will never be repeated! Call
within the next thirty seconds and we will double the offer!
We will add two exercise suits, two pairs of running shoes, and
our exercise movie. You and your partner can run together in
the latest fashions, right there in your game room!"

I grab my phone—then come to my senses, hit the off button, and take a nap.

Snow is still falling the next night, so once again, I settle in
and search for a good movie. I am delighted to see the start of
another of my favorite Sandra Bullock movies, one I haven't
seen in ages. Maybe the pair that ruined last night's movie will
be somewhere else tonight. Oh, no! There are the shining
white letters again.

Nonetheless, I'm determined to watch this movie to the
end. Then, in the first tense and important scene between two
characters, there are the two tiny women again, dressed even
more brightly this time, leaping and mugging. They get right
between the characters, impossible to ignore. But I still watch,
thinking maybe I'll get used to them. I don't.

Why did the Rivers women allow themselves to be demeaned
to this degree? And have the networks no compassion for an
old woman who wants to get lost in a good story? And if the
movie is worth showing, why ruin it by having the jumpers and
pointers invade the characters' space in every important and
beautiful scene? Why, if the duo must jump around because
someone is paying big money to have them there, couldn't they
just spoil a scene when a car is driving down the street, or when
we are looking at mountains in the distance?

I doubt that I will ever watch whatever show Joan and her daughter are carrying on about, but I would watch it if I thought a tiny Sandra Bullock movie would run throughout, down in the right-hand corner of the screen.

# 27

# All Downhill

THE MEMBERS OF THE TALK-SHOW panel on middle age have agreed that with proper diet, exercise, and medical care, the good years have been extended. "Sixty is the new forty," they proclaim. "Seventy is the new fifty."

"Sometimes the good years last until eighty," the host states.

A woman in the audience asks, "What happens after eighty?"

The glib, forty-something host laughs, and says, "It's all downhill after that!"

Everyone laughs.

I gasp and grip the arms of my chair, waiting to drop dead. I'm eighty-eight—surely over the hill, on the downward slope, ready to hit bottom.

There she is, little Glenna, age five, at the playground of the estate where her father works. She loves it when Ann Louise, the little girl who summers there, invites her down to play. Glenna climbs the steps to the top of the slide and looks down the shiny surface, heated by the sun. Sometimes it's so hot she thinks it will burn her bottom, but oh, how she loves the ride. Quickly she climbs the steps again. Mama tells her not to get on the slide because it will wear out her bloomers, but Mama is back running the post office, so she'll just have one more ride. And then another and—the worst that can happen is that if she wears a hole in her bloomers, Mama will tell Papa to give her a spanking. His leather slipper will sting for a few minutes, but the ride is worth the pain.

The scene changes to winter when Glenna is seven and climbing the big hill behind the post office where she lives, pulling her new sled with red letters that spell SPEEDAWAY. Then she's flying down through the soft snow. (I'd call the hill a little knoll now, but it was a big mountain in 1927.)

It's three years later, and both the hill and the sled are longer. The homemade double-runner will hold five or six kids at a time, sometimes each sitting and hugging the person in front, sometimes all lying down and piled helter-skelter. One falls off, causing a pileup, and laughs and squeals. Then back up the hill.

Time passes. Glenna is a college freshman taking a required phys ed course in skiing. She doesn't learn to ski well, but she does master the art of falling down without breaking anything.

Next, the Aroostook farmhouse on a long hill. Back roads are not sanded, and there is almost no traffic in the winter, so the hill is perfect for Don, Glenna, and little sons Steve, Barney, and Mel to have some good fast rides almost to the railroad tracks.

Too soon the boys grow up and go away. Sometimes on a Saturday, Don and Glenna get up early and ski all day at Mont Farlagne. Glenna can manage only the easiest slope, but it is a long, beautiful ride in the sharp, cold air of a sunny winter day.

Last image: Glenna, now living alone, has traded downhill skiing for cross-country. She loves the sounds and smells of the woods, and the occasional little downhill ride.

I no longer ski, but those rides stay with me. Sometimes when I'm listening to music and letting it take me where it will, I'm on Mont Farlagne's toughest slope, all grace and beauty on skis.

All downhill after eighty? What a lovely thought.

# 28

# In a Grain of Sand

AS I LOOK BACK at my more than nine decades, I hope to find some clues that will help me know what life is all about.

When I was four, I remember looking at myself in a full-length mirror at the back of the post office my mother ran. I saw light brown hair, brown eyes, and a face about the same color from the summer sun. That day Mama had sent me out to play in a tan cotton dress. I looked at myself and said, "You're just a big old lump of dirt. You're a big nothing." Constance had pink and white skin, Corris had bangs, Betty had freckles. I had nothing. Yet I was a happy nothing, having all outdoors for my playground, and a world full of stick dolls, rock houses, and imaginary playmates.

A few years later I decided there would be better days ahead when I became the age of those wonderful big people I admired, the high school girls who went to the Saturday-night dances, worked for the summer people, and wore lipstick when their fathers weren't around. Then I'd be free of all these little-kid rules: Don't talk back to your elders; don't take the Lord's name in vain; when you sit, keep your dress down so nobody will see your bloomers; don't make noise while Papa is reading.

When I went to Sullivan High School I found there were as many rules for teenagers as there were for little kids: Don't smoke cigarettes; don't cheat on tests; don't hang around that Jimmy, because his great-grandmother was part Indian.

That was Grammie's rule. Mama's vague but frightening warning was, "There are some mistakes a girl need make but once." She followed that with, "If you lose your good reputation, you'll never get a decent husband." In spite of these restrictions, I enjoyed high school most of the time.

I knew there must be better days ahead, however, and since Papa told me I was going to the University of Maine, I thought that this must be when life gets better—perfect, even. In college, I'd finally be free.

There were a few good things about college. An only child, I finally learned to love being in a dormitory with other girls, some of whom became my friends. I liked going to the stag dances. Since the college at that time had about seven boys for every girl, there was no end of partners. Most of my classes didn't seem to relate to me, but because I had to earn most of my spending money, I learned to be an excellent waitress, and I was proud of that. Once at a banquet I waited on the head table that included Rudy Vallee, the reigning heartthrob at the time.

However, since college wasn't the goal I'd been reaching for, I began to dream of marriage and happily-ever-after.

I soon found that happily-ever-after included worrying about the kids when they were sick, worrying about how we'd pay the mortgage on the farm, and living with guilt because I couldn't seem to find the right balance for doing schoolwork, cooking meals, keeping our clothes in shape, cleaning, and spending enough time with my husband and three sons. Although I enjoyed many of my days, there was always the elusive carrot out there at the end of the stick. *Someday*.

Then one day I found that I was the age of my students' grandparents, that my sons were grown up and didn't need me for much, and that my husband and I had little in common now that the boys were gone. Wait a minute! What about that ideal time in our future? Did I have my best days back there somewhere—and not even know it? On that day before the decline there should have been the blare of trumpets, the roll of drums. But it went by, and I missed it. I began to look back at all the great days past, as looking ahead wasn't all that great.

Finally, life, the old trickster, let me in on the joke. At last I understood the punch line.

I had had it all, all along. Like everyone else, young or old, rich or poor—all any of us have or need is the day we are in. We all start the morning with the same hours out there to use, for daydreaming, loving, sharing, working, creating, learning to be human. Each of my more than thirty thousand days was the best day of my life, at the time.

And here, where I am—it's the best possible place for me to be *at this time.* All the looking ahead and looking back—just smoke and mirrors. I have five senses that still work fairly well, and every day is a feast of sights, sounds, tastes, smells, feelings—yet often I have been the poor fool who didn't even have a spoon. (I'm misquoting Auntie Mame about the spoon.)

When I was little, I woke up happy every day, thinking of what I could do when I went outdoors. Now I wake up happy every day, wondering what I can do that will be fun, and that will somehow justify my existence now, when most of the people in the *Bangor Daily News* obits are younger than I am.

I understand the statistics. I know that some germ or other could take me out at any time. But this morning I have it all.

So far, I have today. I look in the mirror and congratulate the old thing that she made it through another night. Somehow I can get along with myself better than I could in my earlier decades. The lack of self-confidence, the frequent guilty feelings—they don't seem worth the bother anymore.

Now I know that it's okay to do stupid things and fall on my face. It's okay that I can't keep up with younger people in this technological and fast-changing world. I've learned to laugh at my shortcomings. Laughter—that amazing human condition where we fall apart, make strange noises, sometimes shed tears, gasp for breath, and for a moment, forget our aches and pains and the oil bill. I now love every day so much that when it's my time to go, I hope I go with no regrets.

This verse from a William Blake poem is important to me:

To see a world in a grain of sand,
And a heaven in a wild flower,
Hold infinity in the palm of your hand,
And eternity in an hour.

—From *Auguries of Innocence*

# 29

# My List

I JUST HEARD OF A TV CONTEST: Write down what you are thankful for, and you may win a cruise. There is only an online address, so I can't compete, but I keep thinking of what I would write. First and most important: reasonably good health for my age, great family, great friends, and my monthly retirement check.

I'm grateful that all of my senses still work after a fashion, and with the help of triple-vision glasses, eye drops, ear drops, and nose drops. Adding more spices aids my failing sense of taste.

Next, I'd mention my little house on a quiet street with good neighbors—a small space that is crammed full of a lifetime of stuff. But it's my stuff, and I love it.

Then I'd list my dear and spoiled cat, who orders me out of my chair many times a day to do his bidding. Without him I might sit so long I'd get too stiff to move.

I'm grateful for Maine weather: hot and cold, sun and rain, snow and wind. I'd hate to live in a one-climate place.

I'd list the post office steps where I so often happen to meet an old neighbor or a former student not seen for more than fifty years.

And trees. I stare out at them from all my windows in all weather. On my way to the post office I drive by a huge and perfectly proportioned oak. Every day I tell it how beautiful it is. I hope nobody ever takes an ax to it.

139

I'd mention letters and cards written to me by relatives and friends I value. I can save them and read them many times. I can't lose them on my computer. I'd praise old soft sweatshirts and sweatpants. Eighty years ago, women my age wore dresses, corsets, and long stockings hooked to the corsets. Horrible.

I'd have a long list of foods that come from faraway places: oranges, bananas, avocados, and fresh vegetables.

I'm grateful for so many luxuries: refrigerator and freezer, a house with a furnace, running water, and electricity. Then there's my comfortable old chair and my warm bed.

I love the early-morning *Bangor Daily News* that brings me puzzles and word games that get me out of bed when the sun comes up. And then there are playing cards, important since the great-aunts and grammies taught me rummy and double solitaire. I read somewhere that we don't stop playing because we get old—we get old because we stop playing.

Always I've lived in imagination and memory. If I hadn't grown up in the wide empty spaces around my village, and if I had not been surrounded by books, would my imagination have thrived? I doubt it.

My memory plays tricks on me, but I'm glad I have some of it left. Sometimes going back and reliving a day or an hour is more fun than the present—if I'm stuck in a waiting room, for instance, or pushed into a machine for an MRI.

And TV with all of its junk. How my grandparents would have loved watching news, church services, baseball games.

It's a good thing I can't enter that contest. My list is just getting started. I could never have fit it into the number of words allowed. On a day when some of the troubles of old age almost get me down, I just concentrate on my list. Then I say thank-you to the universe for giving me another day.

# Part Four:

# Fiction

# 30

# And a Time to Love

IT WAS UNSEASONABLY WARM FOR MAY—too warm
for sleeping. Doris Bartlett kicked off her blanket, looked at
her glow-in-the-dark clock. One forty-five. She sat up and listened. Her roommate's breathing was heavy, even. She won't
wake up for hours, Doris thought. There was a little slit of
moonlight between the curtains. Even on cloudy nights Doris
always knew when the moon was full because she felt restless,
sad.

Slowly, silently, she went to the bathroom in the dark. She
splashed water on her face, brushed her teeth and her hair,
squirted herself with her favorite cologne. She pulled on the
blue seersucker housecoat, new for her birthday, and opened
the door a crack, her heart pounding. There was no sound,
nobody in sight. On the long trek to the end of the corridor
she stayed close to the wall where the light was dim. Often she
paused to look around and listen. On the way she concocted a
story in case she was caught. "I was having this really amazing
dream. I must have come out of my room in my sleep."

After what seemed hours she reached the long sun porch
at the end of the building. No curtains here—just brilliant
moonlight that made magic of daytime tables, chairs, and
bookcases. She looked around to make sure she was alone,
then went across the room to the window she knew she could
crank out partway. Then there was nothing between her and

the big china-plate moon in its velvet sky. And lilacs! She breathed in their evening fragrance. She was surprised when the town clock struck two. She'd been out of bed for only fifteen minutes.

Then she closed her eyes, doubled her fists, and whispered, "Please, Johnny, wake up and come out here. Oh, please—"

She stared at the far door to the men's wing and waited. Suddenly feeling lonely, she was about to return to her room when the door opened. Was it Johnny? Yes! Neither broke the silence, but she lifted her hand and he answered with a wave.

When he reached her side she said, "I willed you to wake up."

He chuckled. "I know. I felt you tugging at me. I said to my roommate, 'That wild wicked woman won`t let me get any sleep.' "

Doris giggled. "Oh, come on! You didn't say that!" She pulled him closer to the window. "Feel that night air! Look at the moon! Smell the lilacs!"

Just then, as if on cue, they heard soft music from a distance. Somebody somewhere had turned the radio to the all-night nostalgia station. A clarinet played a slow, sad song about a stranger on a shore. Next a soft voice sang "Blue Moon." Johnny and Doris leaned together, swayed to the music.

"In high school I looked at you all the time," Johnny said. "I'd sit a couple of seats back so I could stare at you and still appear to be paying attention to the teacher."

"Why didn't you ever ask me for a date?"

"I didn't dare to," he said. "That Peter Ashe was always tagging you around, and him twice my size and mean-tempered. I was just a scrawny little coward."

"You were tall and slender and gentle," Doris said. "And not a coward. Remember the day Amy Johnson looked out the classroom window and saw two dogs and said, 'Look at those dogs! What are they doing? I think one is hurting the other. Somebody go stop them!' Some boys laughed and teased her, but you stood up for her."

"And you remember that!" he said.

"We'd better go before we get caught," she said.

He touched her face. "You're crying. Why?"

"I don't know—life is so wonderful sometimes. I hate to leave the lilacs."

When he leaned far out the window he could just reach the topmost blossom. He picked it and put it in her hand.

"It's white!" she said. "I pictured it being purple. White ones are my favorite." She pressed the flower to her face. He bent down and kissed her. It may have been the sweetest kiss the old moon had ever witnessed. They parted and went in opposite directions across the big porch. At their doors they paused, looked at each other a few seconds, waved once.

Doris, suddenly fearful, hurried back to her room. She had just closed her door when she heard another door close, footsteps in the hall. She held her breath. The footsteps passed. Quickly she threw off her housecoat and climbed into bed. She dreamed that she and Johnny were running across a big field of daisies and sweetgrass. They clasped hands, laughed, and ran and ran. The sun was in their faces, but there was a cool breeze. They didn't get out of breath; they could have run forever. In the distance they could see the bay. She knew they were going to swim in the green waters when they reached the shore.

But they didn't quite get there, for Doris woke up when her door opened. With her eyes shut tight, she wondered, Is it the nice one? Or the Sparkler? The tread was too heavy for the nice one, and the strident, singsong voice said, "Wake up, my girlies! Almost breakfast time!"

Doris braced herself for the next words, "Rise and shine!" Then the Sparkler gave her a playful slap on the hip. "And were we a naughty girl last night?" Doris opened her eyes to see a finger wagging in her face. Someday I'll bite it, she thought. "Naughty? What do you mean?" she asked.

"You know! Your wheelchair isn't in its right place by the wall. You got up and went to the bathroom without calling a nurse for assistance, didn't you, my girl? We must remember that we recently had hip surgery, and that we're ninety years young. We always call the nurse when we can't sleep."

"I slept well," Doris said. "I had a wonderful dream."

But Miss Sparks wasn't listening. She was walking around the curtain to shed some sunshine on Doris's roommate. Doris made a face at her retreating back. Ninety years old, she muttered. *Old*, you silly ninny. And my hip hurts. I can't digest my favorite foods, and my memory is awful. Oh, I can remember way back, but I don't know what I ate for dinner yesterday. But I'm still real. I'm not a cartoon of a child.

She tried to fall back into the dream. Oh, dear! Was last night—the slow songs, the kiss—a dream, too?

She thrust her hand under her pillow and pulled out the white lilac—bent and withered, but real. She closed her eyes and smiled. When we play cribbage today, she thought, I'll ask Johnny if he parked his chair in the wrong place, too.

# 31

## Libby and Larch

ONLY GEOGRAPHICALLY were they neighbors. They lived in the last two farmhouses far out on the back station road, yet for decades neither had entered the other's home. Only biologically were they cousins; nobody in the village dared mention to either that their fathers were brothers. Both only children and single, they have spent eight decades in the houses where they were raised.

The last time he entered her house was back in the 1940s, the year the river flooded. In the spirit of the moment, he went with some other men to her place to offer to move her to higher ground. She invited them in, served coffee and pumpkin doughnuts, and assured them she'd stay right where she was, thank you very much.

"Might as well let the stubborn old fool drown," Larch muttered as they gave up on their arguments and drove away.

Larch left his home and came back only when it was safe, finding six inches of water standing on his ground floor. Of course the river obliged Libby by falling back before it reached her house.

If the two met face-to-face in the feed store or at town meeting dinner, she'd murmur, "Mornin', Larch," and he'd mutter, "Mornin', Libby," but they had not talked with each other since the big fight in the '30s, when her father, who had got himself educated and who taught in a big college out west, and who according to Larch really thought he was something, demanded his share of the farm where Larch and his father had struggled all those years. Her father and his smart lawyer won, of course. Then in the '50s, one of Larch's hogs got loose, waddled down the road, and rooted up Libby's strawberry patch. She took him to court over that, and he had to pay her seventy-five dollars.

There was nobody left alive who could remind her how proud she was when back in high school he pitched the game that won the county championship; nobody to remind him of how her eyes shone and how her hair blew in the wind when she hung him a May basket and he chased her and caught her and kissed her; nobody to remind either of the horrible day when their mothers said they could no longer play together because they liked each other too much.

"You can't grow up and get married. If cousins marry, their children will be simple."

Resentments grew.

In the '60s, before he knew it was for sale, she bought the strip of land where the brook widened. His favorite fishing hole was along there, but she put up a high fence and NO TRESPASSING signs.

In the '70s there were more skirmishes. Across the road from their farms there was a wooded area where there were patches of the best fiddleheads in the county. The land belonged to a man from the city who didn't care what people did there as long as they didn't cut down the trees. Both Libby and Larch liked to take fiddleheads to the village and sell them to Big Will at the general store. Daily each would check to see if it was picking time. Then on the morning when, armed with buckets and bags, he went out at five o'clock, he'd find that she must have picked the patches clean at four o'clock.

Each decade Larch's frustrations grew, along with his private names for her: uppity old maid, penny-pinching old hag, and "What did I ever do to deserve a lifetime of living near that mean-minded old witch of a woman?"

Then in the '90s Larch struck it lucky. One day at the diner he met up with a man who collected old pop bottles—Moxie, sarsaparilla, birch beer, the earliest Coca-Cola bottles. If they were old he'd pay good money. He said he was covering the walls of his den with them. Larch took the fellow up to his place and showed him the old bottles that had been in the barn for years. He paid Larch two hundred dollars and asked if he could find more. In the next few days Larch visited old and nearly forgotten dumps around the area and found some even more ancient bottles that earned him another hundred. To celebrate his prosperity he ordered a pair of boots from L.L. Bean.

Then he began to hatch a plan that would for once allow him to get the better of Libby. He remembered that in the cellar at her house there were, on a high shelf under the eaves, far more bottles than all he had found. Even when he was a kid they were old and dusty. As highfalutin as she was, Larch doubted that Libby even knew they were there. After all she had done to him, he deserved those bottles. But how to get his hands on them? He could watch, and when she drove by in that big shiny Buick on her way to town, he could go on over in his rusty old pickup—but he suspected that she locked the place up tight whenever she left.

There was an outside cellar door, but it had been boarded up for years, and it would take time for him to get it open.

And if she came back and caught him there, she'd have him in jail for sure. She'd keep him in there for life if she could.

Then one day Billy Hooper, son of Big Will, came by because the Boy Scouts were running a bottle drive. Larch gave the boy what empties he had on hand, and then he asked him if he'd been to the old woman's place up the road. Billy said, "No; I've heard she never lets anyone in."

"Well, maybe she'd let you in if you told her how generous I've been. She doesn't like me much, so she might give you some bottles just to outdo me. And then you could say that if she had any old bottles in the shed or the barn, you'd be glad to clean them out for her. Whatever you do, don't mention the cellar, and don't let on that I put you up to anything." Larch figured that if things went well, he could make some kind of deal with the boy later.

Billy grinned and hurried on over to Libby's place. When she opened the door he stated his errand. She invited him in, gave him a fresh sugared chocolate doughnut and a glass of milk, and found for him a big bag of bottles. Then he ever so casually asked about bottles in the barn or shed, saying that the two boys who brought in the most would win a trip to Portland to watch the Sea Dogs play.

She said she couldn't think of any, but that she'd call him if she found some. He rushed back to report to Larch, whose name he hadn't used at all. He felt like a spy, like one of those secret agents on TV. He also felt guilty because the old woman had been so nice to him. At the supper table Billy told his parents about what had gone on. They laughed. Like most everyone in town, they got a kick out of the Libby-Larch feud.

Larch, meanwhile, made and scrapped several plans for getting his hands on those bottles. Maybe he could get in good

with the man who ran the oil truck. Maybe he could go along
when the fellow cleaned Libby's furnace. But what excuse
could he make for taking the bottles? Maybe he could set a little fire behind Libby's barn and call the fire department. Then,
in all the hubbub, he could get into the cellar and . . .

But somebody might see him. And there are stiff fines for
false calls to the fire department.

There had to be a way. Then one day, while walking past
the drugstore, Larch saw some posters advertising cruises. He
went in and found that the druggist was taking orders for winter trips. Larch gathered up a stack of pamphlets with pictures
of sand and sea and palm trees. Then he waited for a cold,
dark, sleety, windy day, and when Libby drove to town, he
rushed over and put the pamphlets in her mailbox.

He had underlined all references to sales and special deals.
Then, realizing he hadn't seen all those bottles since the 1930s,
he ran over and peered through her cellar window. What if
somebody had taken them already? His heart was pounding. It
was dim in there, but he could see a few of the dusty bottles,
looking just as they did more than sixty years ago.

He waited impatiently to see if Libby would take his bait.
He could rely on Billy for information. Sooner or later everything got talked over at the general store. Finally, after a week
of exceptionally fierce weather, Billy reported that Libby had
told his father one of those cruises surely would be nice, if
only she had someone to milk her cow and look after her
place. Easy as taking candy from a baby, Larch thought.

Larch telephoned Libby that night and told her that if
she wanted to take one of those cruises, he'd be glad to tend
her place, him living so handy. He said that at her age she
deserved to get away once in a while. Larch was only five

months younger than Libby, but he always thought of her as an old woman, and himself as a much younger fellow. Libby gasped, but finally got over the shock enough so she could say, "Why, Larch, how kind of you. I would like to schedule a trip in February if you're sure you don't mind."

Larch rubbed his hands together and giggled every time he thought of February. On the day Libby departed, he even drove her down to the bus stop so she could leave her car home in her garage. Then, although he did not need to tend her animals until evening, he drove right on over. He helped himself to a doughnut since she had urged him to eat them up. Then he sauntered down the cellar stairs, savoring the moment along with the doughnut. He fumbled for the light switch, finally found it, and turned to view his loot. He stared. He stepped closer.

That long, high, almost-hidden shelf was empty. Completely empty. But the bottles had been there just a few weeks ago. What could have happened to them? He couldn't ask around; then people would know what he was up to. He uttered a few cusswords and then did the chores. Twice a day for two weeks he'd have to come over here and do the chores for the old bat, that dried-up prune who was sunning herself in the Bahamas. She always won.

But as the days went by, he found he didn't mind going over there. Her animals seemed glad to see him—the cow, the hens, even her haughty old cat. The place was clean, neat, and homey. It reminded him of Aunt Edna, Libby's mother. He'd loved her when he was little, and he'd loved her cooking. Libby made doughnuts just like her mother's. Sometimes he looked at the snapshot albums in the parlor. There were pictures of him in there. He'd almost forgotten that little boy.

When Libby returned, Larch met her at the station. She thanked him again, saying that the cruise was the experience of a lifetime, and she never could have gone if he hadn't offered his help. She said, "I guess it was meant for me to go; it didn't even cost me anything out of pocket. I'd heard people say you sold your bottles to a fellow from away, so I found his name and called him. I would never have thought about those old bottles under the eaves if the little Hooper boy hadn't come by on a Boy Scout drive. When he asked if I had any old bottles in the barn or anywhere, I finally remembered the ones in the cellar. I went down to see if they were still there. The man paid me enough for them to cover the cost of the cruise."

Larch managed to say, "That's nice," as he realized he'd promoted far more of her trip than she'd ever know.

When he dropped her off he even carried her bags into the house. Early training dies hard. Then she told him that he'd never lack for doughnuts and pie, and that she'd send over stews and casseroles, too, since she always made too much at a time.

As he started out the door she said, "And there's one more thing. Come into the front hall, please." She unlocked a tall cabinet and lifted down two guns—his great-grandfather's Civil War rifle and an even older musket, guns which Larch had coveted for years. "I want you to have these," she said.

When that story made it to the general store, Big Will said to Larch, "They're worth something, too. Way up in the thousands. If you ever want to sell them, I'm in touch with dealers who pay top dollar."

"Oh, I'll never sell them unless I need to, to save the farm," Larch said. "Family stuff is important, you know. My cousin Libby gave them to me."

# 32

## The Carpoolers

AS I TURN ONTO THE RAMP, I yearn to go home to my sweatpants, my cat, and my coffee mug, but it's Thursday. I'll visit my great-uncle, Albert Witham, at the Elms Retreat, an assisted-living complex. He's leaning on his walker, waving and grinning as I drive in.

"Edna!" he yells.

"Unk!" I yell back. I park my car and join him at a picnic table on the side porch. We know an attendant will soon bring iced tea and a plate of cookies. I hope I'll have Unk to myself today.

He glances at me and says, "You look done in. What's the matter?"

"Oh, just the traffic. Took me over an hour to get here. I could make it in twenty minutes in the fast lane, but since that new law—"

"What law?" he asks.

"The one that's supposed to encourage carpooling and cut down on gas use. The one that reserves the fast lane for cars with at least four occupants. And since my schedule is different on some days, I can't find riders."

"Well, that's a stupid law!" Charlie Tracy yells as he joins us.

I try to greet him pleasantly. He and Unk have been close companions all their lives, yet they spend more time fighting than getting along. Gram told me that it started in grade school. Unk, a Catholic, and Charlie, a Methodist, argued on the playground one day about which was the right religion. When they started hitting each other, the teacher dragged them into the schoolhouse and stood them in opposite corners.

They are opposites in many ways—Unk, a lifelong Red Sox fan, while Charlie is a rooter for the Yankees. After the two teams play together, one man gloats and the other sulks. Unk is a Democrat, Charlie, a Republican. Unk says the Democrats are for us little people; Charlie says the Democrats will have us in a Fascist state, the new president, the dictator. Unk can tolerate a good bit of clutter, while Charlie is a neat freak. And so it goes.

Yet they spent all their working years at the same farm machinery company, they married women who were friends, and they lived on the same street. Now widowers, they live two doors away from each other in the Home, and they argue about whose grandson is the best baseball player.

Charlie claps Al on the back and booms, "We'll ride up to the city with you, won't we, Al? We could walk around the park, see a Little League baseball game . . ."

I think, Oh, no! It would be better to be stuck in traffic for an hour. But Uncle Albert is grinning and saying, "Why not? Might be fun, at that. And we could always find a fourth rider." Unk looks happier than I've seen him for a while. I gulp and say, "That's great. I'll pick you up at seven tomorrow."

Next morning the three men, Unk, Charlie, and Bob Morrow, pile into my little Neon, Bob in the front seat with me. We sit quietly while the two in the backseat taunt each other mile after mile.

On the ride home I hear of their adventures in Leavitt Park, the mall and park complex where they wanted to be left for the day. They watched baseball all morning, then ate the brown-bag lunch given them by the cook at the Home. They bought ginger ale at a nearby concession stand.

Unk said, "Old Charlie, the fussbudget, couldn't stand to see the paper plates and cups thrown all over the park, so over he goes to the manager and asks for a big garbage bag. Then he hauls on his white work gloves and picks up trash! I told him that just once I wish he would sit still and enjoy himself. 'They hire people to clean up the trash,' I told him."

Charlie says, "Before my bag was full the owner comes out and thanks me. She says they try to hire boys, but nobody wants the job. She says if I were around every day, she'd pay me. I told her I'd be around sometimes. She's not paying much, but I'll be glad to have a few extra dollars. So now I'm a real carpooler, Edna, with a job. I'll pay you for the ride."

"Oh, no—no need of that," I tell him. I groan to think I'm stuck with him. He goes on and on about having a paying job, unlike some other fellows in the car.

On the next day the third rider is Freda White. She says, "Don't know as I can stand the ride with these two old coots, but it sure will be nice to get away from the Home for a day."

On the way home she told me she walked around the mall and visited a gift shop run by an old friend of hers, and the friend's daughter. She said she found some yarn for a sweater for a granddaughter, and then went to a park bench to knit and watch the people.

"A couple of young mothers sat down near me, one with a toddler, the other with a baby in a carriage. We got to talking, and turns out I knew one girl's grandmother. Small world!

Then they said they'd like to go for a cold drink, but didn't want to push the carriage because the baby would wake up. I said I'd watch the kids and they could both go. I read a book to the toddler. When they came back they brought me an iced tea. They said they wished I'd be there every day, so they could go jogging together. I said I'd be around some days. They said they'd pay me, but of course I refused that."

"Well!" Charlie yells. "Now two of us have jobs, sort of, and only one is unemployable." He kept at Unk all the way home, but Unk remained silent.

When I let them out at the Home, Unk said, "Guess maybe I'll stay home tomorrow, Edna. I'm kind of tired."

I wanted to cry. I wanted to yell at Charlie, but I could think of nothing to say. Freda, who had ridden in silence, patted my hand.

"Don't you worry, dear," she said. Next morning the three of them were there waiting for me, Unk wearing a new maroon sport shirt.

"That shirt looks good on you, Albert," Freda says. Then she turns to me. "You know what Albert and I are going to do tonight? We're going to be partners in the Hearts contest. Albert's a good card player. I shouldn't be surprised if we win the prize."

"Don't count your chickens before they hatch, woman," Charlie says. "My partner and I may have something to say about that."

"Who's your partner?" Unk asks.

"I'm not saying just yet," Charlie mutters.

On the ride home Freda tells me that she persuaded Uncle Albert to let her take some of those jumping jacks that he whittles. She showed them to her friend in the gift shop, and the friend liked them. A few minutes later a man came in and bought two of them for his grandsons.

"So you see, Edna," Freda said, "you now have real carpoolers. I'm an off-and-on babysitter, Charlie picks up all that trash and improves the environment, and now Albert, an artist, is selling his creations."

"Artist!" Charlie snorted. But he couldn't think of an insult.

So the weeks go by and I can stay in the fast lane. When one of my old dears wants a day off, a willing substitute is found. And either I'm getting toughened up, or Unk's and Charlie's arguments are mellowing.

Then I glance at silent little Freda, and I remember a slogan from one of the women's magazines: "Never underestimate the power of a woman."

# About the Author

GLENNA JOHNSON SMITH was born in 1920 in
Ashville, Maine, in coastal Hancock County. She earned a
bachelor's degree in home economics from the University of
Maine in 1941, and with several years of summer and evening
courses, met requirements for majors in social studies and
English literature. That same year she got married and moved
to a farm in Easton, Maine, where she and her husband raised
three sons. She taught English and home economics at schools
in Easton, Fort Fairfield, and Presque Isle, and was heavily
involved in high school and community theater productions.
Presque Isle is now her home.

Her writing has been published in *Echoes* and *Yankee* magazines, and in anthologies, including *Maine Speaks: An Anthology
of Maine Literature*. She has also written a number of award-
winning plays.

She has received numerous other honors as well, including
being named Presque Isle's Citizen of the Year, receiving an
honorary doctorate from the University of Maine–Presque
Isle, and being nominated for the Exemplary Older Person
Award by the state of Maine.